The Pocket Book of
Blessings

The Pocket Book of
Blessings

Inspiring thoughts for
everyday life

ARCTURUS

ARCTURUS

This edition published in 2016 by Arcturus Publishing Limited
26/27 Bickels Yard, 151–153 Bermondsey Street,
London SE1 3HA

Copyright © Arcturus Holdings Limited

ISBN: 978-1-78212-992-9
AD004192NT

Printed in China

Contents

Introduction

Blessings come in all shapes and sizes and often from the most unlikely sources. For some of us a blessing is a gift from God; for others it is an act of nature; or humankind at its most virtuous. All creeds, cultures and philosophies have their own interpretation of blessings but certain criteria seem to apply across the board: blessings are not grandiose, nor are they self-seeking; they cannot be contrived or planned for; they cannot be bought. Blessings should be appreciated and, where possible, returned in kind. Studying blessings reminds us that forgiveness, selflessness, humility and other such traits that go against the competitive mores of modern life, can be more powerful and rewarding than their opposites. This book gathers together hundreds of inspiring quotes to help you find your own definition of blessings – and to find them in your own life.

What a Wonderful World

Look at the trees, look at the birds, look at the clouds, look at the stars... and if you have eyes you will be able to see that the whole of existence is joyful.

Osho

I give you every seed-bearing plant on the face of the whole Earth and every tree that has fruit with seed in it. They will be yours for food.

Genesis 1:29-30

*What spirit is so empty and blind,
that it cannot recognize the fact that
the foot is more noble than the shoe,
and skin more beautiful than the
garment with which it is clothed?*

Michelangelo

**May the rain come down in the proper time,
May the earth yield plenty of corn,
May the country be free from war,
May the Brahmans be secure.**

Hindu prayer

He who is in harmony with Nature hits the mark without effort and apprehends the truth without thinking.

Confucius

A cloudy day or a little sunshine have as great an influence on many constitutions as the most recent blessings or misfortunes.

Joseph Addison

And when you crush an apple with your teeth,
   say to it in your heart:
Your seeds shall live in my body,
And the buds of your tomorrow shall blossom in my heart,
And your fragrance shall be my breath,
And together we shall rejoice through all the seasons.

Khalil Gibran

Here is the great Earth,
Filled with the smell of incense,
Covered with a blanket of flowers,
The Great Mountain, the Four Continents,
Wearing a jewel of the Sun and Moon.
In my mind I make them the Paradise of a Buddha,
And offer it all to You.
By this deed, May every living being
Experience the Pure World.

Tibetan prayer

What a wonderful world you have made out of wet mud, and what beautiful men and women!

Ashanti blessing

May the waters flow peacefully; may the herbs and plants grow peacefully; may all the divine powers bring unto us peace.

Shanti from the Vedas

The colour of the mountains is Buddha's body; the sound of running water is his great speech.

Dogen, Buddhist

When you are in accord with nature, nature will yield up its bounty...and every sacred place is the place where eternity shines through time.

Joseph Campbell

And why do you worry about clothes? See how the lilies of the field grow. They do not labour or spin. Yet I tell you that not even Solomon in all his splendour was dressed like one of these.

Matthew 6:28-29

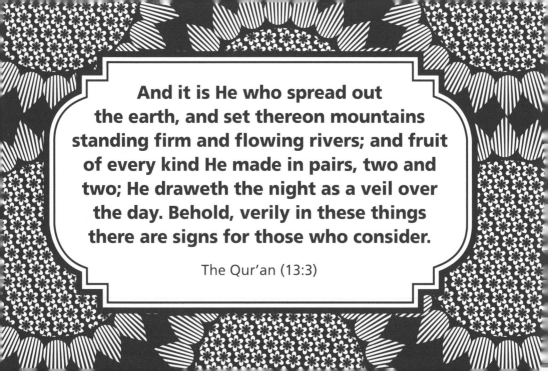

And it is He who spread out the earth, and set thereon mountains standing firm and flowing rivers; and fruit of every kind He made in pairs, two and two; He draweth the night as a veil over the day. Behold, verily in these things there are signs for those who consider.

The Qur'an (13:3)

**The earth is made a place for our prayers,
and its soil is made for our purification.**

Prophet Muhammad

*All that we see – the Heaven,
the Earth, and all that fills it
– all these things are the
external garments of God.*

Rebbe Shneour Zalman

**Fertile soil, level plains, easy passage across
the mountains, coal, iron, and other metals
imbedded in the rocks, and a stimulating
climate, all shower their blessings upon man.**

Ellsworth Huntington

For Equilibrium, a Blessing:
Like the joy of the sea coming home to shore,
May the relief of laughter rinse through
your soul.
As the wind loves to call things to dance,
May your gravity be lightened by grace.
Like the dignity of moonlight restoring the
earth,
May your thoughts incline with reverence
and respect.

As water takes whatever shape it is in,
So free may you be about who you become.
As silence smiles on the other side of what's
  said,
May your sense of irony bring perspective.
As time remains free of all that it frames,
May your mind stay clear of all it names.
May your prayer of listening deepen enough
  to hear in the depths the laughter of god.

John O'Donohue

Humans! They lived in the world where the grass continued to be green and the sun rose every day and flowers regularly turned into fruit, and what impressed them? Weeping statues.

Terry Pratchett, *Small Gods*

Every moment of light and dark is a miracle.

Walt Whitman

Enlightenment is like the moon reflected on the water. The moon does not get wet, nor is the water broken.

Dogen

We gently caress you, the Earth, our planet and our home. Our vision has brought us closer to you, making us aware of the harm we have done to the life-network upon which we ourselves depend. We are reminded that we have poisoned your waters, your lands, your air. We have filled you with the bones of our dead from war and greed. Your pain is our pain.

Buddhist prayer

I have set my rainbow in the clouds, and it will be the sign of the covenant between me and the Earth.

Genesis 9:12-13

In wilderness I sense the miracle of life, and behind it our scientific accomplishments fade to trivia.

Charles Lindbergh

It is only goodness which gives extras, and so I say again that we have much to hope from the flowers.

Arthur Conan Doyle

O! Mother Earth, who has the ocean as clothes and mountains and forests on her body, who is the wife of Lord Vishnu, I bow to you. Please forgive me for touching you with my feet.

Hindu blessing

Look at my creations! See how beautiful and perfect they are! I created everything for you.

Ecclesiastes

Have you not seen how God sends rain down from the sky, making the earth green?

The Qur'an (22:63)

May the good earth be soft under you when you rest upon it, and may it rest easy over you when, at the last, you lay out under it.

Irish blessing

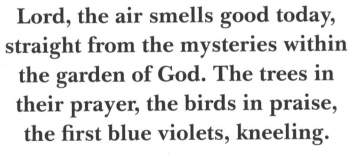

Lord, the air smells good today, straight from the mysteries within the garden of God. The trees in their prayer, the birds in praise, the first blue violets, kneeling.

Rumi

It is He who produces gardens with trellises and without, and dates and tilth with produce of all kinds, and olives and pomegranates similar and different. Eat of their fruit in their season, but render the dues that are proper on the day that the harvest is gathered. And waste not by excess: for Allah loves not the wasters.

Surah 6:141

Let my teaching fall like rain
and my words descend like dew,
like showers on new grass, like
abundant rain on tender plants.

Deuteronomy 32:1-2

May the blessing of the great rains be on you.
May they beat upon your spirit and wash it
fair and clean, and leave there many a shining
pool where the blue of heaven shines,
and sometimes a star.

Irish blessing

Nature's peace will flow into you as sunshine flows into trees.

John Muir (1838–1914)

Sense the blessings of the earth in the perfect arc of a ripe tangerine, the taste of warm, fresh bread, the circling flight of birds, the lavender colour of the sky shining in a late afternoon rain puddle, the million times we pass other beings in our cars and shops and out among the trees without crashing, conflict, or harm.

Jack Kornfield

The brightness of the sun, which lights up the world, the brightness of the moon and of fire – these are my glory. With a drop of my energy I enter the earth and support all creatures. Through the moon, the vessel of life-giving fluid, I nourish all plants.

Lord Krishna

May the rains sweep gentle across your fields.

Irish blessing

It's harvest time, It's harvest time,
How rich is nature's yield
In fruit of earth and bush and tree,
From orchard, farm and field.
It's autumn time, It's autumn time,
When leaves turn gold and red.
In smiling sky and land and sea God's
glories are outspread.

Jewish song

Let us together praise the Lord, from whom we
have rain from the heavens and abundance from
the earth. Blessed be God now and for ever.

Christian prayer

When I walk through thy woods,
May my right foot and my left foot
Be harmless to the little creatures
That move in its grasses: as it is said
By the mouth of thy prophet,
They shall not hurt nor destroy
In all my holy mountain.

Rabbi Moshe Hakotun

If not for the trees,
human life could
not exist.

Midrash Sifre
(Deuteronomy) 20:19

We pray for the healing of our planet that present and future generations may enjoy the fruits of creation, and continue to glorify and praise you.

Christian prayer

Every creature is better alive than dead, men and moose and pine trees, and he who understands it aright will rather preserve its life than destroy it.

Henry David Thoreau

One generation goes and another generation comes; but the earth remains forever.

Ecclesiastes

Nature's beauty is an art of
God. Let us feel the touch
of God's invisible hands
in everything beautiful.

Rig Veda 1.6.3

**Do not stand at my grave and weep,
I am not there... I do not sleep.
I am the thousand winds that blow...
I am the diamond glints on snow...
I am the sunlight on ripened grain...
I am the gentle autumn rain.**

Mary Frye

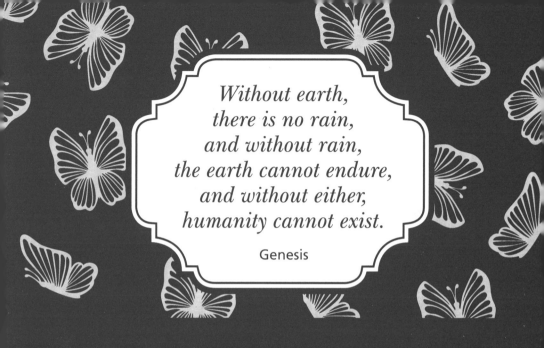

Without earth,
there is no rain,
and without rain,
the earth cannot endure,
and without either,
humanity cannot exist.

Genesis

May the sun bring you new energy by day,
May the moon softly restore you by night,
May the rain wash away your worries,
May the breeze blow new strength into your being,
May you walk gently through the world and
Know it's beauty all the days of your life.

Apache blessing

We are the cosmos made conscious and life is the means by which the universe understands itself.

Brian Cox

If you think this
Universe is bad,
you should see some of
the others.

Philip K. Dick

Give Thanks
and Be Praised

Gratitude is happiness doubled by wonder.

Gilbert K. Chesterton

Those blessings are sweetest that are won with prayer and worn with thanks.

Thomas Goodwin

Keep your eyes open to your mercies. The man who forgets to be thankful has fallen asleep in life.

Robert Louis Stevenson

> *Gratitude bestows reverence... changing forever how we experience life and the world.*
>
> John Milton

May those who enjoy the faithful ministry of the Word feel exceedingly thankful for it. There are few blessings on Earth greater for a believer; and yet the Lord is frequently obliged to teach us the value of this blessing by depriving us of it for a season.

George Muller

Earth provides enough to satisfy every man's need, but not every man's greed.

Mahatma Gandhi

There are only two ways to live your life. One is as though nothing is a miracle. The other is as though everything is a miracle.

Albert Einstein

Miracles are like pimples, because once you start looking for them you find more than you ever dreamed you'd see.

Lemony Snicket

The act is unjustifiable that either begs for a blessing, or, having succeeded, gives no thanksgiving.

Merle Shain

Change your perception of what a miracle is and you'll see them all around you.

Jon Bon Jovi

To take for granted one's blessings is a damage to the soul, and in time one will lose them, simply from lack of care.

Anne Perry

To find one thankful man, I will oblige a great many that are not so.

Seneca

I just thank God for all of the blessings.

James Brown

**God gave you a gift of 84,600 seconds today.
Have you used one of them to say thank you?**

William Arthur Ward

Keep memories of insult on a short leash, and memories of blessing on a long one.

Alan Cohen

*Men are slower to recognize
blessings than misfortunes.*

Livy

Reflect upon your present blessings – of which every man has many – not on your past misfortunes, of which all men have some.

Charles Dickens

Turn your attention for a while away from the worries and anxieties. Remind yourself of all your many blessings.

Ralph Marston

Count your blessings and be grateful, not a great fool.

Habeeb Akande

Of the blessings set before you make your choice, and be content.

Samuel Johnson

What if you gave someone a gift, and they neglected to thank you for it – would you be likely to give them another? Life is the same way. In order to attract more of the blessings that life has to offer, you must truly appreciate what you already have.

Ralph Marston

The worst moment for the atheist is when he is really thankful and has nobody to thank.

Dante Gabriel Rossetti

The only way to live is to accept each minute as an unrepeatable miracle.

Storm Jameson

To witness miracles unfold in your experience, count your blessings and be thankful. Perceived small blessings accumulate to be the most powerful.

T. F. Hodge

Be happy, noble heart, be blessed for all the good thou hast done and wilt do hereafter, and let my gratitude remain in obscurity like your good deeds.

Alexandre Dumas

Be thankful for what you have; you'll end up having more.

Oprah Winfrey

Do not spoil what you have by desiring what you have not; remember that what you now have was once among the things you only hoped for.

Epicurus

Gratitude is not only the greatest of virtues, but the parent of all others.

Cicero

Happy people see blessings where the rest see disappointment.

Anon

Piglet noticed that even though he had a Very Small Heart, it could hold a rather large amount of Gratitude.

A. A. Milne

In this world of sin and sorrow there is always something to be thankful for; as for me, I rejoice that I am not a Republican.

H. L. Mencken

We must find time to stop and thank the people who make a difference in our lives.

John F. Kennedy

Let gratitude be the pillow upon which you kneel to say your nightly prayer.

Maya Angelou

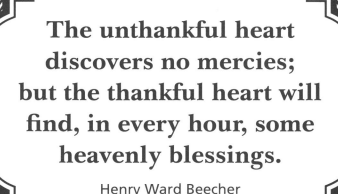

The unthankful heart
discovers no mercies;
but the thankful heart will
find, in every hour, some
heavenly blessings.

Henry Ward Beecher

We can only be said to be alive in
those moments when our hearts
are conscious of our treasures.

Thornton Wilder

Let us be grateful to the mirror for revealing to us our appearance only.

Samuel Butler

**Praise God, from whom all blessings flow!
Praise Him, all creatures here below!
Praise Him above, ye heavenly host!
Praise Father, Son, and Holy Ghost!**

Thomas Ken

Treat the earth well. We do not inherit the earth from our ancestors, we borrow it from our children.

Proverb

Blessed with riches and possibilities far beyond anything imagined by ancestors who tilled the unpredictable soil of medieval Europe, modern populations have nonetheless shown a remarkable capacity to feel that neither who they are nor what they have is quite enough.

Alain de Botton

The drums beat it out, and people sing about it, and they dance with noisy joy that you are the Lord.

Anon

Though I come not within sight of the castle of my dreams, teach me to be thankful for life.

Anon

The highest tribute to the dead is not grief but gratitude.

Thornton Wilder

To live at all is miracle enough.

Mervyn Peake

I wake up every morning now with a smile on my face, thankful for the gift of another day I never expected to see.

Dick Cheney

Thankfulness may consist merely of words. Gratitude is shown in acts.

Henri Frederic Amiel

What a wonderful life I've had! I only wish I'd realized it sooner.

Sidonie Gabrielle Colette

Loving Father and Creator of all, we come to you today deeply grateful for your creation.

Catholic prayer

Remember that not to be happy is not to be grateful.

Elizabeth Carter

Feeling gratitude and not expressing it is like wrapping a present and not giving it.

William Arthur Ward

Can God be counted on? Count blessings and find out how many of His bridges have already held.

Ann Voskamp

Happiness isn't complicated. It is a humble state of gratitude for simple pleasures, tender mercies, recognized blessings, and inherent beauty.

Richelle E. Goodrich

On the recollection of so many and great favours and blessings, I now, with a high sense of gratitude, presume to offer up my sincere thanks to the Almighty, the Creator and Preserver.

William Bartram

Take full account of what excellencies you possess, and in gratitude remember how you would hanker after them, if you had them not.

Marcus Aurelius

Envy is the art of counting
the other fellow's blessings
instead of your own.

Harold Coffin

Happiness is seeing
blessings in disguise,
beauty under camouflage,
and love amid conflict.

Richelle E. Goodrich

Thank God, we're living in a country where
the sky's the limit, the stores are open late
and you can shop in bed thanks to television.

Joan Rivers

There are hundreds of ways to kneel and kiss the earth.

Rumi

Whatever befalls the earth
*   befalls the sons of the earth.*
If men spit upon the ground
*   they spit upon themselves.*

Chief Seattle

I was pirouette and flourish,
I was filigree and flame.
How could I count my blessings
when I didn't know their names?

Rita Dove

I love life because what more is there?

Anthony Hopkins

Drink and be thankful to the host! What seems insignificant when you have it, is important when you need it.

Franz Grillparzer

Such lovely warmth of thought and delicacy of colour are beyond all praise, and equally beyond all thanks!

Marie Corelli

If the only prayer you said was thank you, that would be enough.

Meister Eckhart

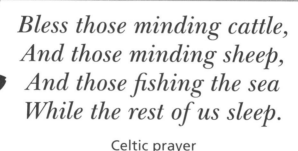

Bless those minding cattle,
And those minding sheep,
And those fishing the sea
While the rest of us sleep.

Celtic prayer

Thank you for the rain. And for the chance to wake up in three hours and go fishing: I thank you for that now, because I won't feel so thankful then.

Garrison Keillor

When you practise gratefulness,
there is a sense of respect
toward others.

The Dalai Lama

We can be thankful to a friend for a few
acres, or a little money; and yet for the
freedom and command of the whole earth,
and for the great benefits of our being,
our life, health, and reason, we look upon
ourselves as under no obligation.

Seneca

The hardest arithmetic to master is that
which enables us to count our blessings.

Eric Hoffer

What a pure blessing it was to have a bath in a tub alone in a room where all you had to do was pump the water, not tote buckets. Then all you had to do was pull out the cork, not tote more buckets to the back porch. That kind of thing is easy to take lightly until you don't have it.

Nancy E. Turner, *Sarah's Quilt*

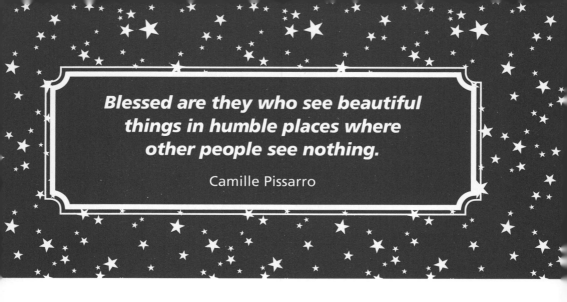

Blessed are they who see beautiful things in humble places where other people see nothing.

Camille Pissarro

When you rise in the morning, give thanks for the light, for your life, for your strength. Give thanks for your food and for the joy of living. If you see no reason to give thanks, the fault lies in yourself.

Tecumseh

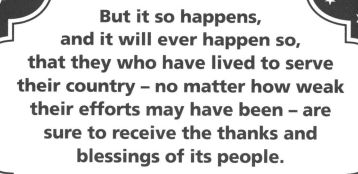

**But it so happens,
and it will ever happen so,
that they who have lived to serve
their country – no matter how weak
their efforts may have been – are
sure to receive the thanks and
blessings of its people.**

Thomas Francis Meagher

*I do not so much rejoice that
God hath made me to be a
Queen, as to be a Queen over
so thankful a people.*

Elizabeth I

I count my blessings every day, quite honestly, because I take nothing for granted.

Mario Andretti

I give all the glory to God. It's kind of a win-win situation. The glory goes up to Him and the blessings fall down on me.

Gabby Douglas

I just find myself happy with the simple things. Appreciating the blessings God gave me.

DMX

I try to be grateful for the abundance of the blessings that I have, for the journey that I'm on and to relish each day as a gift.

James McGreevey

I'm just thankful for everything, all the blessings in my life, trying to stay that way. I think that's the best way to start your day and finish your day. It keeps everything in perspective.

Tim Tebow

We take for granted electricity, water, even concerts. Count your blessings.

Damian Marley

It is so easy to overestimate the importance of our own achievements compared with what we owe to the help of others.

Dietrich Bonhoeffer

Let us be grateful to people who make us happy, they are the charming gardeners who make our souls blossom.

Marcel Proust

God has two dwellings: one in Heaven, and the other in a meek and thankful heart.

Izaak Walton

The degree to which I am blessed staggers me... the degree to which I take that for granted shames me.

John Green

The proud man counts his newspaper clippings, the humble man his blessings.

Fulton J. Sheen

Dear mother earth, who day by day
Unfolds rich blessing on our way,
O praise God! Alleluia!
The fruits and flowers that verdant grow,
Let them his praise abundant show.
O praise God, O praise God,
Alleluia, Alleluia, Alleluia.

Saint Francis of Assisi

A Sense of Enrichment

Blessed are the meek, for they shall inherit the earth.

Jesus

Instead of comparing our lot with that of those who are more fortunate than we are, we should compare it with the lot of the great majority of our fellow men. It then appears that we are among the privileged.

Helen Keller

An aim in life is the only fortune worth finding.

Robert Louis Stevenson

**The future belongs
to those who believe in the
beauty of their dreams.**

Eleanor Roosevelt

*Looking behind, I am filled with gratitude.
Looking forward, I am filled with vision.
Looking upwards, I am filled with strength.
Looking within, I discover peace.*

Apache prayer

May this couple be blessed with an abundance of resources and comforts, and be helpful to one another in all ways.

Hindu marriage blessing

By my troth, niece, thou wilt never get thee a husband, if thou be so shrewd of thy tongue.

William Shakespeare

A sense of blessedness comes from a change of heart, not from more blessings.

Mason Cooley

All the greatest blessings are a source of anxiety, and at no time should fortune be less trusted than when it is best; to maintain prosperity there is need of other prosperity, and on behalf of the prayers that have turned out well we must make still other prayers. For everything that comes to us from chance is unstable, and the higher it rises, the more liable it is to fall.

Seneca

We all look. The lucky find. The wise find.

Nora Roberts

The world owes you nothing. It was here first.

Mark Twain

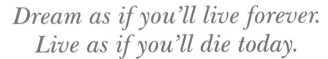

Dream as if you'll live forever. Live as if you'll die today.

James Dean

According to the Sutras, evil deeds result in hardships and good deeds result in blessings.

Bodhidharma

Some are born rich
While others poor;
Some are born free
While others captives;
Some are born blessed
While others deprived;
Some are born strong
While others weak;
And some are born great
While others slaves.
It is only in this life
blessings are unequal.

Emmanuel Aghado

Courage is like love; it must have hope for nourishment.

Napoleon Bonaparte

Riches get their value from the mind of the possessor; they are blessings to those who know how to use them, and curses to those who do not.

Terence

May the blessed sunlight shine on you and warm your heart till it glows like a great peat fire.

Irish blessing

God's arrows of affliction are sharp and painful so He can get our attention. He won't let His beloved children get away with sin because He knows it robs us of blessings, opportunities, and even character refinement.

Charles Stanley

Blessed art Thou, O Lord our God, King of the world who has kept us alive until now so we may find joy in what has just come to us.

Jewish prayer

With the blessings of liberty, we have responsibilities to defend it.

Michael Reagan

With the blessings that God bestowed upon this land came the responsibility to make the world a better place.

Marco Rubio

Man did not weave the web of life – he is merely a strand in it. Whatever he does to the web, he does to himself.

Chief Seattle

You only live once, but if you do it right, once is enough.

Mae West

Two urns on Jove's high throne have ever stood, the source of evil one, and one of good; from thence the cup of mortal man he fills, blessings to these, to those distributes ills; to most he mingles both.

Homer, *The Iliad*

Not life, but good life, is to be chiefly valued.

Socrates

What is important in life is life, and not the result of life.

Johann Wolfgang von Goethe

May the road rise up to meet you.
May the wind always be at your back.
May the sun shine warm upon your face,
And rains fall soft upon your fields.
And until we meet again,
May God hold you in the palm of His hand.

Irish blessing

There is more of value in the brain of an average man of today… than there was in the brain of the world four hundred years ago. These blessings did not fall from the skies. These benefits did not drop from the outstretched hands of priests. They were not found in cathedrals or behind altars, neither were they searched for with holy candles. They were not discovered by the closed eyes of prayer, nor did they come in answer to superstitious supplication. They are the children of freedom, the gifts of reason, observation and experience – and for them all, man is indebted to man.

Robert G. Ingersoll

The Gospel is about grace and we all know that grace is about us receiving from God blessings that we don't deserve.

Tony Campolo

There is nothing to winning, really. That is, if you happen to be blessed with a keen eye, an agile mind, and no scruples whatsoever.

Alfred Hitchcock

Everything that is done in the world is done by hope.

Martin Luther

'We're all blessed and we're all blighted, Chief Inspector,' said Finney. 'Every day each of us does our sums. The question is, what do we count?'

Louise Penny

Don't give up.
Don't lose hope.
Don't sell out.

Christopher Reeve

Be grateful for luck. Pay the thunder no mind – listen to the birds. And don't hate nobody.

Eubie Blake

Life well spent is long.

Leonardo da Vinci

May God be with you and bless you.
May you see your children's children.
May you be poor in misfortunes
and rich in blessings.
May you know nothing but happiness
from this day forward.

Irish marriage blessing

The universe is exactly the size that your soul can encompass.
Some people live in extremely small worlds, and some live in a world of infinite possibility.

Kevin Hearne

For what I have received may the Lord make me truly thankful. And more truly for what I have not received.

Storm Jameson

Death may be the greatest of all human blessings.

Socrates

If we should be blessed by some great reward, such as fame or fortune, it's the fruit of a seed planted by us in the past.

Bodhidharma

A strong mind always hopes, and has always cause to hope.

Thomas Carlyle

Nearly all the best things that came to me in life have been unexpected, unplanned by me.

Carl Sandburg

The greatest blessings of mankind are within us and within our reach. A wise man is content with his lot, whatever it may be, without wishing for what he has not.

Seneca

Talent is God-given. Be humble. Fame is man-given. Be grateful. Conceit is self-given. Be careful.

John Wooden

Talent is not a gift, but a reward for hard work.

Anon

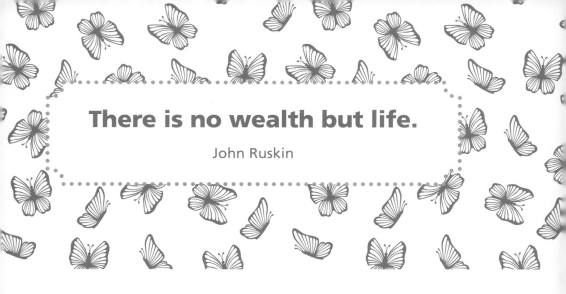

There is no wealth but life.

John Ruskin

Who steals my purse steals trash; 'tis
*   something, nothing;*
'Twas mine, 'tis his, and has been slave to
*   thousands;*
But he that filches from me my good name
Robs me of that which not enriches him,
And makes me poor indeed.

William Shakespeare

Diligence is the mother of good fortune.

Miguel de Cervantes Saavedra

May neighbours respect you,
Trouble neglect you,
The angels protect you,
And heaven accept you.

Irish blessing

A well-spent day brings happy sleep.

Leonardo da Vinci

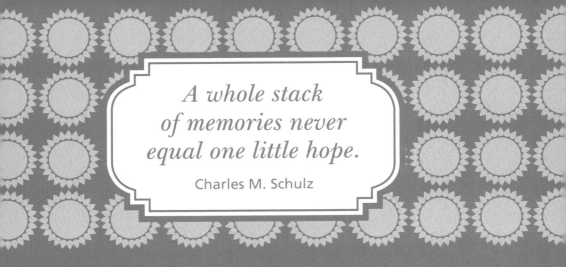

A whole stack of memories never equal one little hope.

Charles M. Schulz

Blessed is the man who has some congenial work, some occupation in which he can put his heart, and which affords a complete outlet to all the forces there are in him.

John Burroughs

A good government remains the greatest of human blessings and no nation has ever enjoyed it.

Dean Inge

I'm most proud of the blessings that God has bestowed upon me. He's given me the vision to truly see that you can fall down, but you can still get back up. Hopefully I'll learn from my mistakes and have the opportunity to strengthen and improve the next thing I do.

Martin Lawrence

Blessed are the forgetful: for they get the better even of their blunders.

Friedrich Nietzsche

If I can find hope anywhere, that's it, that's the best I can do. It's so inadequate but still bless me anyway. I want more life.

Tony Kushner

Every great dream begins with a dreamer.

Harriet Tubman

Change is the law of life. And those who look only to the past or present are certain to miss the future.

John F. Kennedy

Life is a series of natural and spontaneous changes. Don't resist them – that only creates sorrow... Let things flow naturally forward in whatever way they like.

Lao Tzu

Each time we cooperate with God, we take one more giant step forward. Because when God asks us to change, it means that He always has something better to give us – more freedom, greater joy, and greater blessings.

Joyce Meyer

*A miraculous thing
happens when you have
an idea and you want
to convert it into words.*

Janette Turner Hospital

**Birth is the sudden opening of a window,
through which you look out upon a
stupendous prospect... You have exchanged
nothing for the possibility of everything.**

Willie Dixon

**The new always happens against the overwhelming
odds of statistical laws and their probability.**

Hannah Arendt

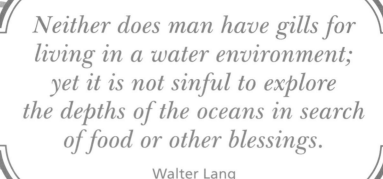

Neither does man have gills for living in a water environment; yet it is not sinful to explore the depths of the oceans in search of food or other blessings.

Walter Lang

We must be willing to let go of the life we have planned, so as to have the life that is waiting for us.

E. M. Forster

It is not the clear-sighted who rule the world. Great achievements are accomplished in a blessed, warm fog.

Joseph Conrad

The internal effects of a mutable policy poisons the blessings of liberty itself.

James Madison

For one swallow does not make a summer, nor does one day; and so too one day, or a short time, does not make a man blessed and happy.

Aristotle

I'm passionately involved in life: I love its change, its colour, its movement.

Arthur Rubinstein

You never know what worse luck your bad luck has saved you from.

Cormac McCarthy, *No Country for Old Men*

Blessed are the people whose leaders can look destiny in the eye without flinching but also without attempting to play God.

Henry A. Kissinger

I'm thankful for the incredible advances in medicine that have taken place during my lifetime.

Billy Graham

All our dreams can come true, if we have the courage to pursue them.

Walt Disney

A man without ambition is dead. A man with ambition but no love is dead. A man with ambition and love for his blessings here on earth is ever so alive.

Pearl Bailey

Experience is growth

Anon

We all make mistakes. The trick is not to let our mistakes make us. Face the music, give thanks for the orchestra and change the tune.

Anon

Without a trace of irony I can say I have been blessed with brilliant enemies. I owe them a great debt, because they redoubled my energies and drove me in new directions.

E. O. Wilson

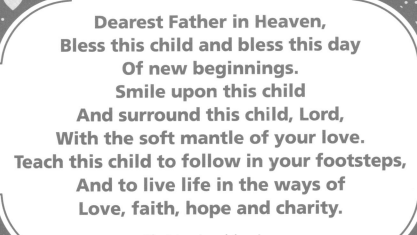

Dearest Father in Heaven,
Bless this child and bless this day
Of new beginnings.
Smile upon this child
And surround this child, Lord,
With the soft mantle of your love.
Teach this child to follow in your footsteps,
And to live life in the ways of
Love, faith, hope and charity.

Christening blessing

*A baby is God's opinion
that life should go on.*

Carl Sandburg

**The child must know
that he is a miracle,
that since the beginning
of the world there hasn't
been, and until the end of
the world there will not be,
another child like him.**

Pablo Casals

**Our prayers should be for blessings in general,
for God knows best what is good for us.**

Socrates

We pray that henceforth not only Japan but all mankind may know the blessings of harmony and progress.

Shigeru Yoshida

I hope that I may always desire more than I can accomplish.

Michelangelo

If one advances confidently in the direction of his dreams, and endeavours to live the life which he has imagined, he will meet with success unexpected in common hours.

Henry David Thoreau

Hope is the thing with feathers that perches in the soul – and sings the tunes without the words – and never stops at all.

Emily Dickinson

Learn from yesterday, live for today, hope for tomorrow. The important thing is not to stop questioning.

Albert Einstein

A healthful hunger for a great idea is the beauty and blessedness of life.

Jean Ingelow

> **Blessed is he who expects nothing, for he shall never be disappointed.**
>
> Jonathan Swift

We must accept finite disappointment, but never lose infinite hope.

Martin Luther King, Jr.

I find hope in the darkest of days, and focus in the brightest. I do not judge the universe.

Dalai Lama

A life is not important except in the impact it has on other lives.

Jackie Robinson

Lord save us all from a hope tree that has lost the faculty of putting out blossoms.

Mark Twain

Three grand essentials
to happiness in this life are
something to do, something
to love, and something
to hope for.

Joseph Addison

I'm trying to look at my blessings and how amazingly well against all odds things have turned out for me.

James Taylor

Hope is the dream of a waking man.

Aristotle

History has shown us that courage can be contagious and hope can take on a life of its own.

Michelle Obama

Good health and good sense are two of life's greatest blessings.

Publilius Syrus

Be careful to leave your sons well instructed rather than rich, for the hopes of the instructed are better than the wealth of the ignorant.

Epictetus

We have always held to the hope, the belief, the conviction that there is a better life, a better world, beyond the horizon.

Franklin D. Roosevelt

On balance, my life has been a constant stream of blessings rather than disappointments and failures and tragedies.

Jimmy Carter

To affect the quality of the day, that is the highest of arts.

Henry David Thoreau

Hope is like the sun, which, as we journey toward it, casts the shadow of our burden behind us.

Samuel Smiles

Anything that just costs money is cheap.

John Steinbeck

**Good friends, good books and a
sleepy conscience: this is the ideal life.**

Mark Twain

*Over and over I marvel at the blessings of my
life: each year has grown better than the last.*

Lawrence Welk

Three meals plus bedtime make four sure blessings a day.

Mason Cooley

Blessed are the hearts that can bend; they shall never be broken.

Albert Camus

> **Blessed is he who has found his work; let him ask no other blessedness.**
>
> Thomas Carlyle

I've got a fantastic life. I enjoy what I do for a living. I see the blessings; I'm not blind.

Anon

The thankful receiver bears a plentiful harvest.

William Blake

Don't let people become your burden. If the ties of the past pull you back, cut them free and spring forward to a brighter future and feel the blessing of merciful release.

Anon

Until we meet again, may God bless you as he has blessed me.

Elvis Presley

Hope springs eternal in the human breast: Man never is, but always to be Blest.

Alexander Pope

Know your own value to God: in your humility, keep in mind that you matter enough to ask Him the question and are worthy of the blessing of a reply.

Anon

You're blessed if you have the strength to work.

Mahalia Jackson

You can relive your past as many times as you like, the experience will never change. Embrace the influence you have on now.

Anon

Don't block your blessings. Don't let doubt stop you from getting where you want to be.

Jennifer Hudson

It's the growth within that matters. For it is the riches of the soul that give true joy and cannot be robbed away.

Anon

It is not by being richer or more powerful that a man becomes better; one is a matter of fortune, the other of virtue.

Héloïse d'Argenteuil

*Never deprive someone of hope;
it might be all they have.*

H. Jackson Brown, Jr.

*Don't aim for success if
you want it; just do what
you love and believe in,
and it will come naturally.*

David Frost

Seek first his kingdom and his
righteousness, and all these things
will be given to you as well.

Matthew 6:33

You will never be happy if you continue to search for what happiness consists of. You will never live if you are looking for the meaning of life.

Albert Camus

Go confidently in the direction of your dreams.
Live the life you have imagined.

Henry David Thoreau

Yesterday is but today's memory, and tomorrow is today's dream.

Khalil Gibran

> **It is one of the blessings of this world that few people see visions and dream dreams.**
>
> Zora Neale Hurston

Perceived small blessings accumulate to be the most powerful.

T. F. Hodge

To succeed in life, you need two things: ignorance and confidence.

Mark Twain

Nothing builds self-esteem and self-confidence like accomplishment.

Thomas Carlyle

Material blessings, when they pay beyond the category of need, are weirdly fruitful of headache.

Philip Wylie

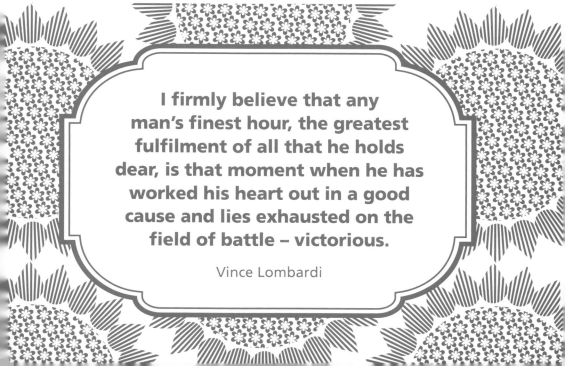

I firmly believe that any man's finest hour, the greatest fulfilment of all that he holds dear, is that moment when he has worked his heart out in a good cause and lies exhausted on the field of battle – victorious.

Vince Lombardi

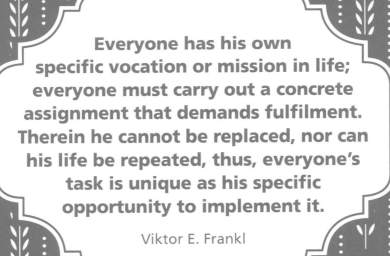

Everyone has his own specific vocation or mission in life; everyone must carry out a concrete assignment that demands fulfilment. Therein he cannot be replaced, nor can his life be repeated, thus, everyone's task is unique as his specific opportunity to implement it.

Viktor E. Frankl

It is not in the pursuit of happiness that we find fulfilment, it is in the happiness of pursuit.

Denis Waitley

The chief condition on which, life, health and vigor depend is action. It is by action that an organism develops its faculties, increases its energy, and attains the fulfilment of its destiny.

Colin Powell

Acting provides the fulfilment of never being fulfilled. You're never as good as you'd like to be. So there's always something to hope for.

Washington Irving

I have wandered all my life, and I have also travelled; the difference between the two being this, that we wander for distraction, but we travel for fulfilment.

Hilaire Belloc

Coming together is a beginning; keeping together is progress; working together is success.

Henry Ford

Life finds its purpose and fulfilment in the expansion of happiness.

Maharishi Mahesh Yogi

There is no fulfilment in things whatsoever. And I think one of the reasons that depression reigns supreme amongst the rich and famous is some of them thought that maybe those things would bring them happiness. But what, in fact, does is having a cause, having a passion. And that's really what gives life's true meaning.

Benjamin Carson

Desire increases when fulfilment is postponed.

Pierre Corneille

We all want progress, but if you're on the wrong road, progress means doing an about-turn and walking back to the right road; in that case, the man who turns back soonest is the most progressive.

C. S. Lewis

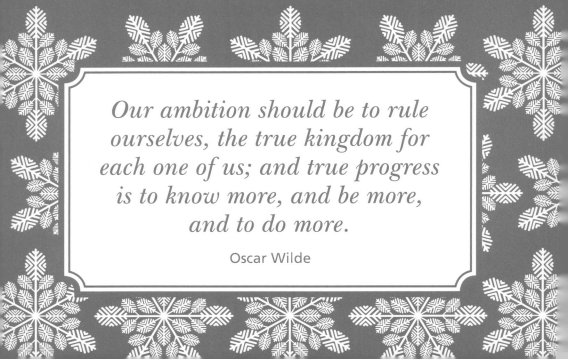

Our ambition should be to rule ourselves, the true kingdom for each one of us; and true progress is to know more, and be more, and to do more.

Oscar Wilde

Honest disagreement is often a good sign of progress.

Mahatma Gandhi

You were put on this earth to achieve your greatest self, to live out your purpose, and to do it fearlessly.

Steve Maraboli

Progress lies not in enhancing what is, but in advancing toward what will be.

Khalil Gibran

Action and reaction, ebb and flow, trial and error, change – this is the rhythm of living. Out of our over-confidence, fear; out of our fear, clearer vision, fresh hope. And out of hope, progress.

Bruce Barton

America and Islam are not exclusive and need not be in competition. Instead, they overlap, and share common principles of justice and progress, tolerance and the dignity of all human beings.

Barack Obama

Political chaos is connected with the decay of language... one can probably bring about some improvement by starting at the verbal end.

George Orwell

The best road to progress is freedom's road.

John F. Kennedy

We cannot seek achievement for ourselves and forget about progress and prosperity for our community... Our ambitions must be broad enough to include the aspirations and needs of others, for their sakes and for our own.

Cesar Chavez

Healthy discontent is the prelude to progress.

Mahatma Gandhi

The improvement of understanding is for two ends: first, our own increase of knowledge; secondly, to enable us to deliver that knowledge to others.

John Locke

He who busies himself with things other than improvement of his own self becomes perplexed in darkness and entangled in ruin. His evil spirits immerse him deep in vices and make his bad actions seem handsome.

Ali ibn Abi Talib

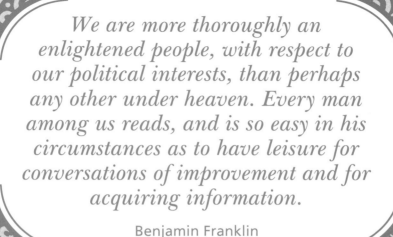

We are more thoroughly an enlightened people, with respect to our political interests, than perhaps any other under heaven. Every man among us reads, and is so easy in his circumstances as to have leisure for conversations of improvement and for acquiring information.

Benjamin Franklin

He who asks of life nothing but the improvement of his own nature... is less liable than anyone else to miss and waste life.

Henri Frederic Amiel

To improve is to change; to be perfect is to change often.

Winston Churchill

The best security for civilization is the dwelling, and upon properly appointed and becoming dwellings depends, more than anything else, the improvement of mankind.

Benjamin Disraeli

I arise in the morning torn between a desire to improve the world and a desire to enjoy the world. This makes it hard to plan the day.

E. B. White

In order to improve the mind, we ought less to learn, than to contemplate.

René Descartes

How wonderful it is that nobody need wait a single moment before starting to improve the world.

Anne Frank

Look not mournfully into the past, it comes not back again. Wisely improve the present, it is thine. Go forth to meet the shadowy future without fear and with a manly heart.

Henry Wadsworth Longfellow

Doubt, the essential preliminary of all improvement and discovery, must accompany the stages of man's onward progress. The faculty of doubting and questioning, without which those of comparison and judgment would be useless, is itself a divine prerogative of the reason.

Albert Pike

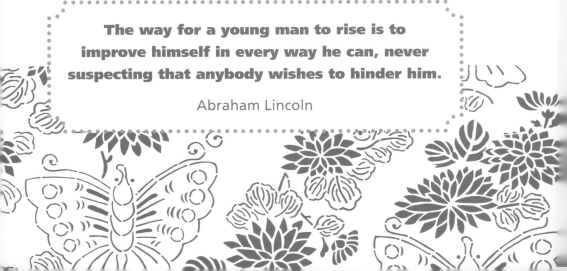

The way for a young man to rise is to improve himself in every way he can, never suspecting that anybody wishes to hinder him.

Abraham Lincoln

Far better is it to dare mighty things, to win glorious triumphs, even though chequered by failure... than to rank with those poor spirits who neither enjoy nor suffer much, because they live in a gray twilight that knows not victory nor defeat.

Theodore Roosevelt

Have want for only that which you need and you may declare your life a success indeed.

Anon

It is better to conquer yourself than to win a thousand battles. Then the victory is yours. It cannot be taken from you, not by angels or by demons, heaven or hell.

Buddha

May every good seed you
have planted bear fruit,
and late summer find you
standing in fields of plenty.

Irish blessing

A Life of
Virtue

Ponnammal set the example for the others by quietly doing what they did not care to do. Her spirit created a new climate in the place, and the time came when there was not one nurse who would refuse to do whatever needed to be done.

Elisabeth Elliot

Courtesies of a small and trivial character are the ones which strike deepest in the grateful and appreciating heart.

Henry Clay

All of us are born with a letter from God written on the very edge of our heart. When we are true to ourselves and others, one day we will be allowed to read it before we die.

Shannon L. Alder

True happiness is not attained through self-gratification, but through fidelity to a worthy purpose.

Helen Keller

The blessings we evoke for
another descend upon ourselves.

Edmund Gibson

All the blessings we enjoy are Divine deposits,
committed to our trust on this condition, that they
should be dispensed for the benefit of our neighbours.

John Calvin

Manipulation, fuelled with good
intent, can be a blessing. But when
used wickedly, it is the beginning of
a magician's karmic calamity.

T. F. Hodge

My own experience about all the blessings I've had in my life is that the more I give away, the more that comes back. That is the way life works, and that is the way energy works.

Ken Blanchard

The inherent vice of capitalism is the unequal sharing of blessings; the inherent virtue of socialism is the equal sharing of miseries.

Winston Churchill

When you wish someone joy, you wish them peace, love, prosperity, happiness... all the good things.

Maya Angelou

Good Morning! Good Afternoon! Good Night! These are not just mere greetings. They are powerful blessings, setting the best vibration for the day. Hence, whether it is morning, afternoon or night, make sure that you say your greeting right!

Franco Santoro

Count your blessings and remember those who have made the ultimate sacrifice for all of us and for freedom.

Anon

If you expect the blessings of God, be kind to His people.

Abu Bakr

Give and you will be blessed.

Joel Osteen

Never undertake anything for which you wouldn't have the courage to ask the blessings of heaven.

Georg C. Lichtenberg

I am a link in Lord Buddha's golden chain of love that stretches around the world. I must keep my link bright and strong. I will try to be kind and gentle to every living thing, and protect all who are weaker than myself.

Buddhist prayer

Seek not greater wealth,
but simpler pleasure;
not higher fortune,
but deeper felicity.

Mahatma Gandhi

Quit smoking and observe posted speed limits. This will improve your odds of getting old enough to be wise.

Barbara Kingsolver

Unless we make Christmas an occasion to share our blessings, all the snow in Alaska won't make it 'white'.

Bing Crosby

Evoking the presence of great compassion, let us fill our hearts with our own compassion – towards ourselves and towards all living beings.

Buddhist prayer

With pride, there are many curses.
With humility, there come many blessings.

Ezra Taft Benson

I will try to think pure and beautiful thoughts, to say pure and beautiful words, and to do pure and beautiful deeds, knowing that on what I do now depends my happiness and misery.

Buddhist prayer

If you are really thankful, what do you do? You share.

W. Clement Stone

May I be a lamp in the darkness
A resting place for the weary
A healing medicine for all who are sick
A vase of plenty, a tree of miracles.

Buddhist prayer

When we give cheerfully and accept gratefully, everyone is blessed.

Maya Angelou

> *The price of anything is the amount of life you exchange for it.*
>
> Henry David Thoreau

Do all the good you can. By all the means you can. In all the ways you can. In all the places you can. At all the times you can. To all the people you can. As long as ever you can.

John Wesley

Make us worthy, Lord, to serve our fellow men throughout the world who live and die in poverty and hunger. Give them through our hands this day their daily bread, and by our understanding love, give peace and joy.

Mother Teresa

If someone as blessed as I am is not willing to clean out the barn, who will?

Ross Perot

May I be a guard for those who
need protection
A guide for those on the path
A boat, a raft, a bridge for those
who wish to cross the flood.

Buddhist prayer

**Let not the needy be
forgotten, nor the hope of
the poor be taken away.
Make us instruments of
your peace and let your
glory be over all the earth.**

Church of England prayer

May our hearts be filled with compassion for others and for ourselves.

Buddhist prayer

Never elated when someone's oppressed, never dejected when another one's blessed.

Alexander Pope

Words have the power to both destroy and heal. When words are both true and kind, they can change our world.

Buddha

Blessed are the merciful, for they shall obtain mercy.

Jesus

Life becomes harder for us when we live for others, but it also becomes richer and happier.

Albert Schweitzer

Blessed are they who hunger and thirst for righteousness, for they shall be satisfied.

Jesus

And may the blessing of the Earth be upon you, the great round earth. May you ever have a kindly greeting for them you pass.

Anon

May we always be ready to help those in need, whoever they are and wherever they may be.

UK scouting prayer

If you try another's shoes and they cause you pain, throw them away. Why should anyone wear shoes that hurt?

Anon

I slept and dreamt that life was joy.
I awoke and saw that life was service.
I acted and behold, service was joy.

Rabindranath Tagore

Lord, clothe me with the robes of innocence.

Anon

Let us never shame any person on earth, great or small. May it be granted unto us to fulfil Thy Commandment to 'Love thy neighbour as thyself', with all our hearts and souls and bodies and possessions.

Jewish prayer

Only a life lived for others is a life worthwhile.

Albert Einstein

Blessed are the pure of heart, for they shall see God.

Jesus

There is a blessed necessity by which the interest of men is always driving them to the right; and, again, making all crime mean and ugly.

Ralph Waldo Emerson

Life has meaning only if one barters it day by day for something other than itself.

Antoine de Saint-Exupéry

**Look upon your children
   that they may face the
   winds.
And walk the good road
   to the Day of Quiet.**

Sioux prayer

*All my ambition is, I own,
To profit and to please unknown;
Like streams supplied from springs below
Which scatter blessings as they go.*

Charles Cotton

> If you wish to glimpse inside a human soul and get to know a man, don't bother analyzing his ways of being silent, of talking, of weeping, of seeing how much he is moved by noble ideas; you will get better results if you just watch him laugh. If he laughs well, he's a good man.

Fyodor Dostoyevsky

Life is a long lesson in humility.

J. M. Barrie

Life appears to me too short to be spent in nursing animosity, or registering wrongs.

Charlotte Brontë

Forgiveness is the answer to
the child's dream of a miracle
by which what is broken is
made whole again, what is
soiled is made clean again.

Dag Hammarskjöld

*Could a greater miracle take place
than for us to look through each
other's eyes for an instant?*

Henry David Thoreau

A miracle is a child donating all the money in their piggy bank to help victims of Hurricane Katrina. That's where you'll find the hand and face of God.

Cathie Linz

The miracle is not that we do this work, but that we are happy to do it.

Mother Teresa

It is not doing the thing we like to do, but liking the thing we have to do, that makes life blessed.

Johann Wolfgang von Goethe

Kind words are a creative force, a power that concurs in the building up of all that is good, an energy that showers blessings upon the world.

Lawrence G. Lovasik

Every person who will learn the right way, and who will then continue diligently to follow that right way, is absolutely certain in time to possess great riches and all attending blessings.

Joseph Franklin Rutherford

The miracle is this: the more we share the more we have.

Leonard Nimoy

To live a pure unselfish life, one must count nothing as one's own in the midst of abundance.

Buddha

Blessed are those who give without remembering. And blessed are those who take without forgetting.

Bernard Meltzer

Blessed is he who has learned to admire but not envy, to follow but not imitate, to praise but not flatter, and to lead but not manipulate.

William Arthur Ward

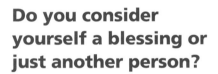

Do you consider yourself a blessing or just another person?

Jonathan Anthony Burkett

God grant me the courage not to give up what I think is right even though I think it is hopeless.

Chester W. Nimitz

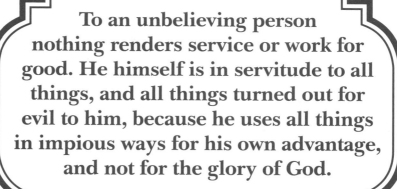

> To an unbelieving person nothing renders service or work for good. He himself is in servitude to all things, and all things turned out for evil to him, because he uses all things in impious ways for his own advantage, and not for the glory of God.
>
> Martin Luther

Man can never be a woman's equal in the spirit of selfless service with which nature has endowed her.

Mahatma Gandhi

Others may trample on you and think themselves blessed for their power, but in seeking such a blessing they are cursed and it is you who are blessed.

Anon

I am in the habit of looking not so much to the nature of a gift as to the spirit in which it is offered.

Robert Louis Stevenson

Let us sacrifice our today so that our children can have a better tomorrow.

Abdul Kalam

To thine own self be true, and it must follow, as the night the day, thou canst not then be false to any man.

William Shakespeare

I count him braver who overcomes his desires than him who conquers his enemies; for the hardest victory is over self.

Aristotle

It is not enough to say we must not wage war. It is necessary to love peace and sacrifice for it.

Martin Luther King, Jr.

Can anything be so elegant as to have few wants, and to serve them one's self?

Ralph Waldo Emerson

> *Excellence is an art won by training and habituation. We do not act rightly because we have virtue or excellence, but we rather have those because we have acted rightly. We are what we repeatedly do. Excellence, then, is not an act but a habit.*
>
> Aristotle

*Virtue consists, not in abstaining
from vice, but in not desiring it.*

George Bernard Shaw

**There is no austerity equal to a balanced
mind, and there is no happiness equal
to contentment; there is no disease like
covetousness, and no virtue like mercy.**

Chanakya

**Virtue is not left to stand
alone. He who practises
it will have neighbours.**

Confucius

*Just as treasures are uncovered
from the earth, so virtue
appears from good deeds,
and wisdom appears from a
pure and peaceful mind.*

Buddha

**Forgiveness is a
virtue of the brave.**

Indira Gandhi

Blessings in Adversity

> **As the blessings of health and fortune have a beginning, so they must also find an end. Everything rises but to fall, and increases but to decay.**
>
> Sallust

The Lord bestows his blessings there, where he finds the vessels empty.

Thomas à Kempis

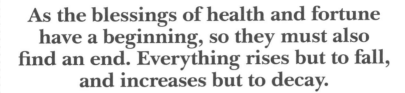

Any adversity you endure is merely the setting of the scene for all your blessings to play out.

Anon

Our real blessings often appear to us in the shape of pains, losses and disappointments; but let us have patience and we soon shall see them in proper figures.

Joseph Addison

May we be strengthened with the understanding that being blessed does not mean that we shall always be spared all the disappointments and difficulties of life.

Heber J. Grant

Blessings sometimes show up in unrecognizable disguises.

Janette Oke

Even seasonal situations can bring with them lessons that last a lifetime. If the love doesn't last, it prepares you for the one that will.

Mandy Hale

I think in every lesson there's a blessing, and there's so many blessings from all the lessons I've had to go through in life.

Alonzo Mourning

The shadow proves the sunshine.

Anon

*We all want relationships
that are healthy and resolved,
and sometimes that simply
doesn't happen. But the
beauty of life is that inside
these disappointments are
hidden the most miraculous
of blessings. What we lose
and what we might have been
pales against what we have.*

Laura Schroff

When life is good and we have no problems, we can almost let ourselves believe we have no need for God. But in my experience, sometimes the richest blessings come through pain and hard things.

Anne Graham Lotz

Spare yourself the torture of raking over the past, but use the lessons well. Nothing in your past is wasted. It all prepares you for now.

Anon

When we lose one blessing, another is often most unexpectedly given in its place.

C. S. Lewis

Those who expect to reap the blessings of freedom, must, like men, undergo the fatigues of supporting it.

Thomas Paine

If we never experience the chill of a dark winter, it is very unlikely that we will ever cherish the warmth of a bright summer's day.

Anthon St Maarten

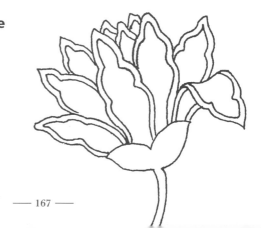

Remember when life's path is steep to keep your mind even.

Horace

***Suffer not thy wrongs to shroud thy fate
But turn, my soul, to blessings which remain.***

Anna Seward

We often look so long and so regretfully upon the closed door that we do not see the one that has opened for us.

Alexander Graham Bell

Don't cry because it's over, smile because it happened.

Dr Seuss

For a life blessed and rewarded with dignity, watch your Ts and Cs: grateful when your star is shining, graceful when it dims.

Anon

Nothing stimulates our appetite for the simple joys of life more than the starvation caused by sadness or desperation.

Anthon St Maarten

May all beings everywhere plagued with sufferings of body and mind quickly be freed from their illnesses.

Buddhist prayer

Blessed are they who are persecuted for the sake of righteousness, for theirs is the kingdom of heaven.

Jesus

When I hear somebody sigh, 'Life is hard,' I am always tempted to ask, 'Compared to what?'

Sydney J. Harris

In order to complete our amazing life journey successfully, it is vital that we turn each and every dark tear into a pearl of wisdom, and find the blessing in every curse.

Anthon St Maarten

God the Father, by whose glory Christ was raised from the dead, strengthen you to walk with him in his risen life.

Holy Communion blessing

**May those frightened cease to be afraid,
and may those bound be free.**

Buddhist prayer

**We are always in a hurry to be happy...
for when we have suffered a long
time, we have great difficulty in
believing in good fortune.**

Alexandre Dumas

*Bad times have a scientific value.
These are occasions a good
learner would not miss.*

Ralph Waldo Emerson

Whatever good or bad fortune may come our way we can always give it meaning and transform it into something of value.

Hermann Hesse

Blessed are the poor in spirit, for theirs is the kingdom of heaven. Blessed are they who mourn, for they shall be comforted.

Jesus

Life is a succession of lessons which must be lived to be understood.

Helen Keller

Life is not a problem to be solved, but a reality to be experienced.

Søren Kierkegaard

How blessed are some people, whose lives have no fears, no dreads; to whom sleep is a blessing that comes nightly, and brings nothing but sweet dreams.

Bram Stoker

Love of God is pure when joy and suffering inspire an equal degree of gratitude.

Simone Weil, *Gravity and Grace*

Misfortune is a stepping stone for genius, the baptismal font of Christians, treasure for the skilful man, an abyss for the feeble.

Honoré de Balzac

The greatest glory in living lies not in never falling, but in rising every time we fall.

Ralph Waldo Emerson

True forgiveness is when you can say, 'Thank you for that experience.'

Oprah Winfrey

Don't shrink from fear but see it as a challenge, an opportunity for progress. When you have learned to embrace fear, than you can begin to grow.

Anon

People living deeply have no fear of death.

Anaïs Nin

Who of you by worrying can add a single hour to his life?

Matthew 6:27

If God sends you down a stony path, may he give you strong shoes.

Irish blessing

May God give you...
For every storm, a rainbow,
For every tear, a smile,
For every care, a promise,
And a blessing in each trial.
For every problem life sends,
A faithful friend to share,
For every sigh, a sweet song,
And an answer for each prayer.

Irish blessing

Who will tell whether one happy moment of love or the joy of breathing or walking on a bright morning and smelling the fresh air, is not worth all the suffering and effort which life implies.

Erich Fromm

The courage of life is often a less dramatic spectacle than the courage of a final moment; but it is no less a magnificent mixture of triumph and tragedy.

John F. Kennedy

If you don't die of thirst,
there are blessings in the desert.

Anne Lamott

Sometimes we have to hit bottom before we figure out how to really enjoy life.

Michael Palmer, *Miracle Cure*

You pray in your distress and in your need;
would that you might pray also in the fullness
of your joy and in your days of abundance.

Khalil Gibran, *The Prophet*

May you see God's light on the path ahead
When the road you walk is dark.
May you always hear, even in your hour
   of sorrow,
The gentle singing of the lark.
When times are hard may hardness
Never turn your heart to stone,
May you always remember when the
   shadows fall
You do not walk alone.

Irish blessing

Those who expect to reap the blessings of freedom must, like men, undergo the fatigue of supporting it.

Thomas Paine

A few years' experience will convince us that those things which at the time they happened we regarded as our greatest misfortunes have proved our greatest blessings.

George Mason

Maybe all one can do is hope to end up with the right regrets.

Arthur Miller

Was memory always as much of a burden as it could sometimes be a blessing.

Mary Balogh

A miracle is nothing more than dormant justice from another time arriving to compensate those it has cruelly abandoned. Whoever knows this is willing to suffer, for he knows that nothing is in vain.

Mark Helprin, *Winter's Tale*

All the art of living lies in a fine mingling of letting go and holding on.

Havelock Ellis

Now is the time to understand more, so that we may fear less.

Marie Curie

A wise man should consider that health is the greatest of human blessings, and learn how by his own thought to derive benefit from his illnesses.

Hippocrates

There may be reasons why we ought to be thankful for even those dispensations which appear dark and frowning.

Albert Barnes

One city gives you gifts, another robs you. One gives you the heart's affections, the other destroys your soul.

Roman Payne

This morning of the small snow I count the blessings, the leak in the faucet which makes of the sink time, the drop of the water on water.

Charles Olson

Some people come in our life as blessings. Some come in your life as lessons.

Mother Teresa

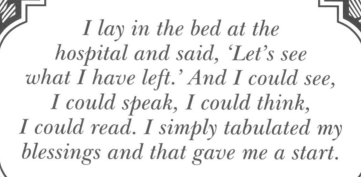

I lay in the bed at the hospital and said, 'Let's see what I have left.' And I could see, I could speak, I could think, I could read. I simply tabulated my blessings and that gave me a start.

Dale Evans

We must free ourselves of the hope that the sea will ever rest. We must learn to sail in high winds.

Aristotle Onassis

Sometimes our light goes out but is blown into flame by another human being.

Albert Schweitzer

For the boundless multitudes of living beings
May I bring sustenance and awakening
Enduring like the earth and sky
Until all beings are freed from sorrow
And all are awakened.

Buddhist prayer

Those born to wealth, and who have the means of gratifying every wish, know not what is the real happiness of life, just as those who have been tossed on the stormy waters of the ocean on a few frail planks can alone realize the blessings of fair weather.

Alexandre Dumas

I shall the effect of this good lesson keep, As watchman to my heart.

William Shakespeare

Better a diamond with a flaw than a pebble without.

Confucius

If you must hold yourself up to your children as an object lesson, hold yourself up as a warning and not as an example.

George Bernard Shaw

By three methods we may learn wisdom: First, by reflection, which is noblest; Second, by imitation, which is easiest; and third by experience, which is the bitterest.

Confucius

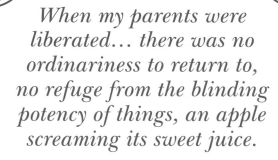

When my parents were liberated… there was no ordinariness to return to, no refuge from the blinding potency of things, an apple screaming its sweet juice.

Anne Michaels

There is no better than adversity. Every defeat, every heartbreak, every loss, contains its own seed, its own lesson on how to improve your performance the next time.

Malcolm X

Experience: that most brutal of teachers. But you learn, my God do you learn.

C. S. Lewis

A wise man can learn more from a foolish question than a fool can learn from a wise answer.

Bruce Lee

Uncertainty is a sign of humility, and humility is just the ability or the willingness to learn.

Charlie Sheen

The quest for certainty blocks the search for meaning. Uncertainty is the very condition to impel man to unfold his powers.

Erich Fromm

Some people grumble that roses have thorns; I am grateful that thorns have roses.

Alphonse Karr

We could never learn to be brave and patient if there were only joy in the world.

Helen Keller

Realize that illness and other temporal setbacks often come to us from the hand of God our Lord, and are sent to help us know ourselves better, to free ourselves of the love of created things, and to reflect on the brevity of this life and, thus, to prepare ourselves for the life which is without end.

Saint Ignatius

Modest doubt is called the beacon of the wise.

William Shakespeare

Sense and Spirituality

May the light shine out of the two eyes of you like a candle set in the windows of a house, bidding the wanderer to come in out of the storm.

Gaelic blessing

I offer you peace. I offer you love. I offer you friendship. I see your beauty. I hear your need. I feel your feelings.

Mahatma Gandhi

While there's life, there's hope.

Marcus Tullius Cicero

Give us the strength to understand,
   and the eyes to see.
Teach us to walk the soft Earth as
   relatives to all that live.

Sioux prayer

Poetry is the spontaneous overflow of powerful feelings: it takes its origin from emotion recollected in tranquillity.

William Wordsworth

*Let the beauty we love
be what we do.*

Rumi

Open my eyes, God. Help me to perceive what I have ignored, to uncover what I have forgotten, to find what I have been searching for. Remind me that I don't have to journey far to discover something new, for miracles surround me, blessings and holiness abound. And You are near. Amen.

Naomi Levy

Feelings, whether of compassion or irritation, should be welcomed, recognized, and treated on an absolutely equal basis; because both are ourselves.

Thích Nhất Hạnh

Life is far too important a thing ever to talk seriously about.

Oscar Wilde

Life does not cease to be funny when people die any more than it ceases to be serious when people laugh.

George Bernard Shaw

May love and laughter light your days, and warm your heart and home.

Irish blessing

The grace of your creation is like a cool day between rainy seasons.

Ashanti blessing

When we remember we are all mad, the mysteries disappear and life stands explained.

Mark Twain

The miracle of your mind isn't that you can see the world as it is. It's that you can see the world as it isn't.

Kathryn Schulz

Blessed is he who lights up the lives of others with the spirit of laughter.

Anon

We are all here for a spell, get all the good laughs you can.

Will Rogers

***The aim of life is to live, and to
live means to be aware, joyously,
drunkenly, serenely, divinely aware.***

Henry Miller

Dance like no one is watching.

Anon

What do we live for, if it is not to make life less difficult to each other?

George Eliot, *Middlemarch*

Instead of beating myself up for being fat, I think it's a miracle that I laugh every day and walk through my life with pride.

Camryn Manheim

To live is so startling it leaves little time for anything else.

Emily Dickinson

Sing! Sing with all your heart! Even when you don't know the words. Keep singing!

Anon

Though everything else may appear shallow and repulsive, even the smallest task in music is so absorbing, and carries us so far away from town, country, earth, and all worldly things, that it is truly a blessed gift of God.

Felix Mendelssohn

…we hardly realize any more that a book can be valuable, valuable like a jewel, or a lovely picture, into which you can look deeper and deeper and get a more profound experience every time.

D. H. Lawrence

All are agreed, that the increase of learning and good morals are great blessings to society.

Joseph Lancaster

The love of learning,
the sequestered nooks,
And all the sweet serenity of books.

Henry Wadsworth Longfellow

Beautiful music is the art of the prophets that can calm the agitations of the soul; it is one of the most magnificent and delightful presents God has given us.

Martin Luther

Sometimes I feel I am really blessed to be blind because I probably would not last a minute if I were able to see things.

Stevie Wonder

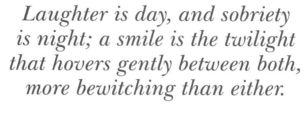

Laughter is day, and sobriety is night; a smile is the twilight that hovers gently between both, more bewitching than either.

Henry Ward Beecher

My great hope is to laugh as much as I cry.

Maya Angelou

Laughter is not at all a bad beginning for a friendship, and it is far the best ending for one.

Oscar Wilde

Remember me with smiles and laughter, for that is how I will remember you all. If you can only remember me with tears, then don't remember me at all.

Laura Ingalls Wilder

Through humour, you can soften some of the worst blows that life delivers.

Bill Cosby

Humour is emotional chaos remembered in tranquility.

James Thurber

A day without laughter
is a day wasted.

Charlie Chaplin

With mirth and laughter let old wrinkles come.

William Shakespeare

I am thankful for laughter, except
when milk comes out of my nose.

Woody Allen

Youth is happy because it has the capacity to see beauty. Anyone who keeps the ability to see beauty never grows old.

Franz Kafka

A man should hear a little music, read a little poetry, and see a fine picture every day of his life, in order that worldly cares may not obliterate the sense of the beautiful which God has implanted in the human soul.

Johann Wolfgang von Goethe

A thing of beauty is a joy forever.

John Keats, *Endymion: A Poetic Romance*

Summer afternoon – summer afternoon; to me those have always been the two most beautiful words in the English language.

Henry James

Everything has beauty, but not everyone sees it.

Confucius

Think of all the beauty still left around you and be happy.

Anne Frank

The human race has one really effective weapon, and that is laughter.

Mark Twain

Laughter is the sun that drives winter from the human face.

Victor Hugo

> **Do I love you because you're beautiful,
> or are you beautiful because I love you?**
>
> Richard Rodgers

The power of finding beauty in the humblest things makes home happy and life lovely.

Louisa May Alcott

**Beauty is eternity gazing at itself in a mirror.
But you are the eternity and you are the mirror.**

Khalil Gibran

The art of living is more like wrestling than dancing.

Marcus Aurelius

Music is a moral law. It gives soul to the universe, wings to the mind, flight to the imagination, and charm and gaiety to life and to everything.

Plato

Music expresses that which cannot be said and on which it is impossible to be silent.

Victor Hugo

The best and most beautiful things in the world cannot be seen or even touched. They must be felt with the heart.

Helen Keller

Music in the soul can be heard by the universe.

Lao Tzu

He who draws noble delights from sentiments of poetry is a true poet, though he has never written a line in all his life.

George Sand

Music is everybody's possession. It's only publishers who think that people own it.

John Lennon

Next to the Word of God, the noble art of music is the greatest treasure in the world.

Martin Luther

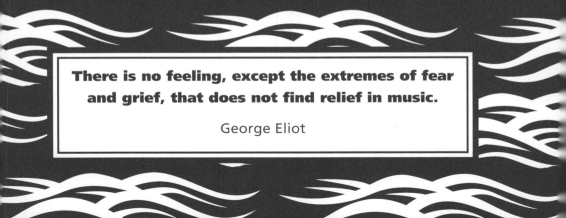

There is no feeling, except the extremes of fear and grief, that does not find relief in music.

George Eliot

To see clearly is poetry, prophecy and religion all in one.

John Ruskin

Any healthy man can go without food for two days – but not without poetry.

Charles Baudelaire

One should sympathize with the colour, the beauty, the joy of life. The less said about life's sores the better.

Oscar Wilde

A table, a chair, a bowl of fruit and a violin: what else does a man need to be happy?

Albert Einstein

It's often just enough to be with someone.

Marilyn Monroe

Everything has its wonders, even darkness and silence, and I learn, whatever state I may be in, therein to be content.

Helen Keller

Health is the greatest gift, contentment the greatest wealth, faithfulness the best relationship.

Buddha

Small enlightenment will bring great enlightenment. If you breathe in and are aware that you are alive... then that is a kind of enlightenment.

Thích Nhãt Hạnh

It is the supreme art of the teacher to awaken joy in creative expression and knowledge.

Albert Einstein

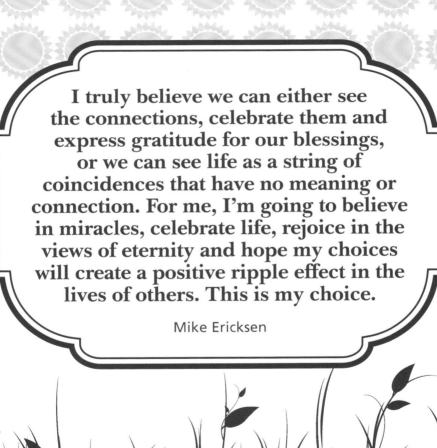

I truly believe we can either see the connections, celebrate them and express gratitude for our blessings, or we can see life as a string of coincidences that have no meaning or connection. For me, I'm going to believe in miracles, celebrate life, rejoice in the views of eternity and hope my choices will create a positive ripple effect in the lives of others. This is my choice.

Mike Ericksen

Just because you can explain it doesn't mean it's not still a miracle.

Terry Pratchett

Our rational minds often attempt to minimize or negate the mystical encounters. We forget the power of our experiences.

Brian Weiss

If miracles had chemical equations then everyone would believe.

Cecelia Ahern

When the mind is pure, joy follows like a shadow that never leaves.

Buddha

However many blessings we expect from God, His infinite liberality will always exceed all our wishes and our thoughts.

John Calvin

Participation in the blessings of the union with Christ comes when the faithful have all the things needed to live well and blessedly to God.

William Ames

Money can't buy no blessins.

Ron Hall

Sometimes God makes better choices for us than we could have ever made for ourselves.

Jennifer Hudson Taylor

There is nothing but mystery in the world, how it hides behind the fabric of our poor, browbeat days, shining brightly, and we don't even know it.

Sue Monk Kidd

If you tell God no because He won't explain the reason He wants you to do something, you are actually hindering His blessing. But when you say yes to Him, all of heaven opens to pour out His goodness and reward your obedience. What matters more than material blessings are the things He is teaching us in our spirit.

Charles Stanley

If we are to be blessed, we must pursue the Giver of blessings.

Dillon Burroughs

If you believe in God, He will open the windows of heaven and pour blessings upon you.

Mahalia Jackson

It becomes us in humility to make our devout acknowledgments to the Supreme Ruler of the Universe for the inestimable civil and religious blessings with which we are favoured.

James K. Polk

When we . . . read and study the scriptures, benefits and blessings of many kinds come to us. This is the most profitable of all study in which we could engage.

Howard W. Hunter

Look at the birds of the air; they do not sow or reap or store away in barns, and yet your heavenly Father feeds them. Are you not much more valuable than they?

Jesus

We must let go of the life we have planned, so as to accept the one that is waiting for us.

Joseph Campbell

Grant that we may be spiritually one, both within ourselves and with one another.

Christian prayer

May God, who in Christ gives us a spring of water welling up to eternal life, perfect in you the image of his glory.

Holy Communion blessing

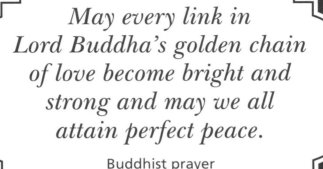

*May every link in
Lord Buddha's golden chain
of love become bright and
strong and may we all
attain perfect peace.*

Buddhist prayer

Almighty God... guide with Your pure and
peaceable wisdom those who make decisions for
the nations of the earth; that in tranquillity Your
kingdom may go forward, till the earth be filled
with the knowledge of Your love.

Anon

> # The whole earth has been made a mosque and pure for me.
>
> Bukhari

The voices of the loved ones reveal to us that you are in our midst. A divine voice sings through all creation.

Jewish prayer

To those leaning on the sustaining infinite, today is big with blessings.

Mary Baker Eddy

Before the world was created, the Holy One kept creating worlds and destroying them. Finally, He created this one and was satisfied. He said to Adam: 'This is the last world I shall make. I place it in your hands: hold it in trust.'

Anon

The God of hope fill you with all joy and peace in believing.

Holy Communion blessing

'Blessings be on this house,' Granny said, perfunctorily. It was always a good opening remark for a witch. It concentrated people's minds on what other things might be on this house.

Terry Pratchett

Any artist should be grateful for a naive grace which puts him beyond the need to reason elaborately.

Saul Bellow

Not knowing is what drives me on.

Anon

The God of all grace, who called you to his eternal glory in Christ Jesus, establish, strengthen and settle you in the faith.

Holy Communion blessing

We pray for all who come here this evening.
Although differences in thought and belief divide us,
Let the desire to serve you,
The love of truth
And the pursuit of holiness unite us.

Prayer

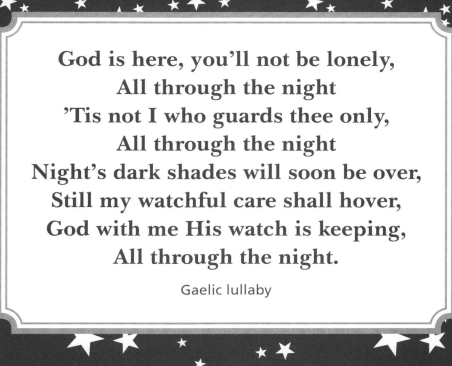

God is here, you'll not be lonely,
All through the night
'Tis not I who guards thee only,
All through the night
Night's dark shades will soon be over,
Still my watchful care shall hover,
God with me His watch is keeping,
All through the night.

Gaelic lullaby

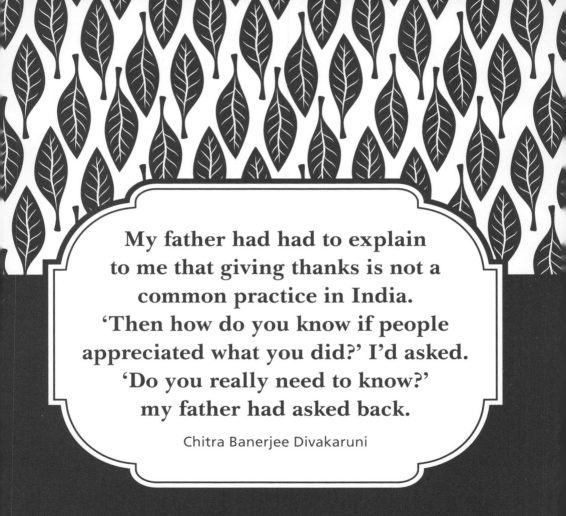

My father had had to explain
to me that giving thanks is not a
common practice in India.
'Then how do you know if people
appreciated what you did?' I'd asked.
'Do you really need to know?'
my father had asked back.

Chitra Banerjee Divakaruni

May the Father, from whom every family in Earth and Heaven receives its name, strengthen you with his Spirit in your inner being, so that Christ may dwell in your hearts by faith.

Holy Communion blessing

Creating the world, God has made it a place to practise spirituality.

Guru Granth Sahib

Blessed be childhood, which brings down something of heaven into the midst of our rough earthliness.

Henri Frederic Amiel

Christ in the heart of every man
  who thinks of me
Christ in the mouth of every man
  who speaks of me
Christ in every eye that sees me
Christ in every ear that hears me
Salvation is of the Lord.

From Saint Patrick's breastplate

I applaud anything that can take a kid
away from a PlayStation or a Gameboy.

Gary Oldman

Miracles are a retelling in small letters of the very same story which is written across the whole world in letters too large for some of us to see.

C. S. Lewis

If patience is worth anything, it must endure to the end of time. And a living faith will last in the midst of the blackest storm.

Mahatma Gandhi

I am thankful I can see much to admire in all religions.

Alfred Russel Wallace

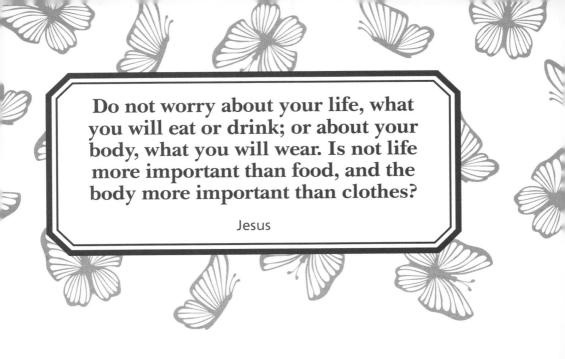

> **Do not worry about your life, what you will eat or drink; or about your body, what you will wear. Is not life more important than food, and the body more important than clothes?**
>
> Jesus

I believe the ability to think is blessed. If you can think about a situation, you can deal with it. The big struggle is to keep your head clear enough to think.

Richard Pryor

The Bible is one of the greatest blessings bestowed by God on the children of men. It has God for its author; salvation for its end, and truth without any mixture for its matter. It is all pure.

John Locke

Faith is a knowledge within the heart, beyond the reach of proof.

Khalil Gibran

Faith is taking the first step even when you don't see the whole staircase.

Martin Luther King, Jr.

Woe to the makers of literal translations, who by rendering every word weaken the meaning! It is indeed by so doing that we can say the letter kills and the spirit gives life.

Voltaire

There are only two forces in the world, the sword and the spirit. In the long run the sword will always be conquered by the spirit.

Napoleon Bonaparte

Doubt is a pain too lonely to know that faith is his twin brother.

Khalil Gibran

Faith is the strength by which a shattered world shall emerge into the light.

Helen Keller

Faith is to believe what you do not see; the reward of this faith is to see what you believe.

Saint Augustine

I gave in, and admitted that God was God.

C. S. Lewis

Man is made by his belief. As he believes, so he is.

Johann Wolfgang von Goethe

I love you when you bow in your mosque, kneel in your temple, pray in your church. For you and I are sons of one religion, and it is the spirit.

Khalil Gibran

There are no constraints on the human mind, no walls around the human spirit, no barriers to our progress except those we ourselves erect.

Ronald Reagan

> **Where the spirit does not work with the hand, there is no art.**
>
> Leonardo da Vinci

It is not so much for its beauty that the forest makes a claim upon men's hearts, as for that subtle something, that quality of air that emanation from old trees, that so wonderfully changes and renews a weary spirit.

Robert Louis Stevenson

Someone who thinks the world is always cheating him is right. He is missing that wonderful feeling of trust in someone or something.

Eric Hoffer

It's the repetition of affirmations that leads to belief. And once that belief becomes a deep conviction, things begin to happen.

Muhammad Ali

Belief is a wise wager.

Blaise Pascal

Humans are amphibians – half spirit and half animal. As spirits they belong to the eternal world, but as animals they inhabit time.

C. S. Lewis

Let parents bequeath to their children not riches, but the spirit of reverence.

Plato

There is no definition of beauty, but when you can see someone's spirit coming through, something unexplainable, that's beautiful to me.

Liv Tyler

Once we believe in ourselves, we can risk curiosity, wonder, spontaneous delight, or any experience that reveals the human spirit.

e. e. cummings

If you want to accomplish the goals of your life, you have to begin with the spirit.

Oprah Winfrey

O Holy Spirit, descend plentifully into my heart. Enlighten the dark corners of this neglected dwelling and scatter there Thy cheerful beams.

Saint Augustine

Now, God be praised, that to believing souls gives light in darkness, comfort in despair.

William Shakespeare

There is no logical way to the discovery of these elemental laws. There is only the way of intuition, which is helped by a feeling for the order lying behind the appearance.

Albert Einstein

Wonder is the feeling of the philosopher, and philosophy begins in wonder.

Plato

Be faithful in small things because it is in them that your strength lies.

Mother Teresa

All who call on God in true faith, earnestly from the heart, will certainly be heard, and will receive what they have asked and desired.

Martin Luther

God always takes the simplest way.

Albert Einstein

May all I say and all I think
Be in harmony with thee,
God within me,
God beyond me,
Maker of the trees.

Chinook prayer

Your spirit is the true shield.

Morihei Ueshiba

Happiness dwells in the soul.

Democritus

**It is better in prayer
to have a heart
without words than
words without a heart.**

Mahatma Gandhi

A man would rather leave behind him the portrait of his spirit than a portrait of his face.

Robert Louis Stevenson

***The Great Spirit is our Father, but the Earth is
our Mother. She nourishes us, that which we
put into the ground, She returns to us...***

Big Thunder

In your soul are infinitely precious things that cannot be taken from you.

Oscar Wilde

The mountains, I become a part of it…
The herbs, the fir tree, I become a part of it.
The morning mists, the clouds,
the gathering waters,
I become a part of it.
The wilderness, the dew drops, the pollen…
I become a part of it.

Navajo chant

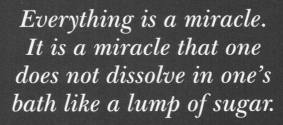

Everything is a miracle.
It is a miracle that one
does not dissolve in one's
bath like a lump of sugar.

Pablo Picasso

Yet it is in this loneliness that the deepest activities begin. It is here that you discover act without motion, labour that is profound repose, vision in obscurity, and, beyond all desire, a fulfilment whose limits extend to infinity.

Thomas Merton

Death is the mother of Beauty; hence from her, alone, shall come fulfilment to our dreams and our desires.

Wallace Stevens

Only on paper has humanity yet achieved glory, beauty, truth, knowledge, virtue and abiding love.

George Bernard Shaw

Faith keeps many doubts in her pay. If I could not doubt, I should not believe.

Henry David Thoreau

Uncertainty is the refuge of hope.

Henri Frederic Amiel

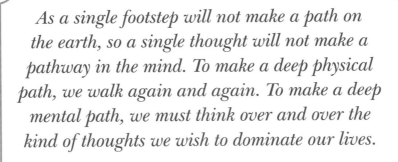

As a single footstep will not make a path on the earth, so a single thought will not make a pathway in the mind. To make a deep physical path, we walk again and again. To make a deep mental path, we must think over and over the kind of thoughts we wish to dominate our lives.

Henry David Thoreau

My faith is one that admits some doubt.

Barack Obama

A little thought and a little kindness are often worth more than a great deal of money.

John Ruskin

I want it said of me by those who knew me best, that I always plucked a thistle and planted a flower where I thought a flower would grow.

Abraham Lincoln

The glow of one warm thought is to me worth more than money.

Thomas Jefferson

If you read history you will find that the Christians who did most for the present world were precisely those who thought most of the next. It is since Christians have largely ceased to think of the other world that they have become so ineffective in this.

C. S. Lewis

The Universe has shouted itself alive. We are one of the shouts.

Ray Bradbury

Self-expression must pass into communication for its fulfilment.

Pearl S. Buck

I think, at a child's birth, if a mother could ask a fairy godmother to endow it with the most useful gift, that gift should be curiosity.

Eleanor Roosevelt

If we are to go forward, we must go back and rediscover those precious values – that all reality hinges on moral foundations and that all reality has spiritual control.

Martin Luther King, Jr.

*Thought is the wind,
knowledge the sail,
and mankind
the vessel.*

Augustus Hare

While I thought that I was learning how to live, I have been learning how to die.

Leonardo da Vinci

Maybe Christmas, the Grinch thought, doesn't come from a store.

Dr Seuss

Make Your Blessings Count

Every day holds the possibility of a miracle.

Elizabeth David

In reality, serendipity accounts for one per cent of the blessings we receive in life, work and love. The other 99 per cent is due to our efforts.

Peter McWilliams

When we do the best that we can, we never know what miracle is wrought in our life, or in the life of another.

Helen Keller

How blessings brighten as they take their flight.

Edward Young

> Life is short, Break the Rules.
> Forgive quickly, Kiss SLOWLY.
> Love truly. Laugh uncontrollably
> And never regret ANYTHING
> That makes you smile.
>
> Mark Twain

Be the peace you wish for the world.

Mahatma Gandhi

Be true to yourself, help others, make each day your masterpiece, make friendship a fine art, drink deeply from good books – especially the Bible, build a shelter against a rainy day, give thanks for your blessings and pray for guidance every day.

John Wooden

Begin at once to live, and count each separate day as a separate life.

Seneca

Don't give up 15 minutes before the miracle comes. Everyone's career ebbs and flows... That's the time to dig in and keep your instrument sharp.

Erik King

You have it in your power to make your days on Earth a path of flowers, instead of a path of thorns.

Sri Sathya Sai Baba

When we quit playing Hokey Pokey with God and keep our whole self in, His blessings pursue us!

Evinda Lepins

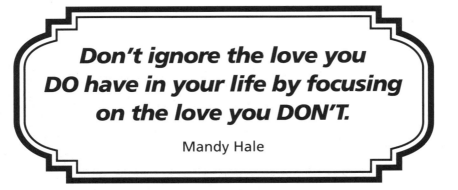

Don't count your blessings, let your blessings count! Enjoy Life!

Bernard Kelvin Clive

> *Don't ignore the love you DO have in your life by focusing on the love you DON'T.*
>
> Mandy Hale

Don't wish...DO!
Don't try...BE!
Don't think...KNOW!
And above all: bless a
stranger with a small,
yet powerful, random
act of kindness.

T. F. Hodge

There are untold joys awaiting
you when you stop caring about
what others think and start living
the life you've been blessed with.

Anon

If you raise your children to feel that they can accomplish any goal or task they decide upon, you will have succeeded as a parent and you will have given your children the greatest of all blessings.

Brian Tracy

Night time brings the joy of anticipation: the anticipation of a new dawn and the discovery of the new blessing that comes my way.

Anon

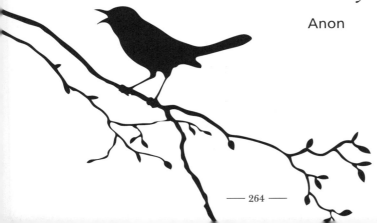

A man who dares to waste one hour of time has not discovered the value of life.

Charles Darwin

Once you discover that you can, then you must. And it's not easy. You have to take direct steps. You really have to count your blessings and you have to make a decided effort to not get seduced by the blues.

Al Jarreau

> **There is no greatness where there is no simplicity, goodness and truth.**
>
> Leo Tolstoy

For the happiest life, days should be rigorously planned, nights left open to chance.

Mignon McLaughlin

Deny the challenge that faces you and you ignore opportunity. Only by accepting the challenge can you conquer it and discover the blessings it conceals.

Anon

Be realistic: plan for a miracle.

Osho

You have to participate relentlessly in the manifestations of your own blessings. And once you have achieved a state of happiness, you must never become lax about maintaining it, you must make a mighty effort to keep swimming upward into that happiness forever, to stay afloat on top of it.

Elizabeth Gilbert, *Eat, Pray, Love*

Restraint equals indulgence.

Barbara Kingsolver

Life consists not in holding good cards but in playing those you hold well.

Josh Billings

Life loves the liver of it.

Maya Angelou

Life must be lived as a play, playing certain games, making sacrifices, singing and dancing, and then a man will be able to propitiate the gods and defend himself against his enemies, and win in the contest.

Plato

May you live all the days of your life.

Jonathan Swift

Old age is not a matter for sorrow, it is a matter for thanks if we have left our work done behind us.

Thomas Carlyle

The miracle is not to walk on water. The miracle is to walk on the green earth, dwelling deeply in the present moment and feeling truly alive.

Thích Nhất Hạnh

One of the main aims in life is to enjoy it.

Samuel Butler

Look upon life as a duty and it will pass you by. Look upon it as an adventure and it will carry you along to untold heights.

Anon

The true secret of happiness lies in taking a genuine interest in all the details of daily life.

William Morris

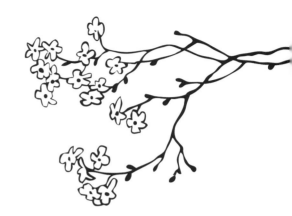

Use your health, even to the point of wearing it out. That is what it is for. Spend all you have before you die; do not outlive yourself.

George Bernard Shaw

Change your life today. Don't gamble on the future, act now, without delay.

Simone de Beauvoir

We can't plan life. All we can do is be available for it.

Lauryn Hill

When I stand before God at the end of my life, I would hope that I would not have a single bit of talent left, and could say, 'I used everything you gave me.'

Erma Bombeck

Live the actual moment.
Only this moment is life.

Thích Nhất Hạnh

Unbeing dead isn't being alive.

e. e. cummings

The greatest discovery of my generation is that a human being can alter his life by altering his attitudes.

William James

There are three constants in life... change, choice and principles.

Stephen Covey

Regardless of your emotions, whether happy or sad, confident or insecure, you remain the sole driver of your actions. Life is up to you.

Anon

**For each new dawn is filled
with infinite possibilities for new
beginnings and new discoveries.
Life is constantly changing and
renewing itself. In this new day of new
beginnings with God, all things are
possible. We are restored and renewed
in a joyous awakening to the wonder
that our lives are and yet can be.**

Christian prayer

If you live long enough, you'll make mistakes.

Bill Clinton

A life spent making mistakes is not only more honourable, but more useful than a life spent doing nothing.

George Bernard Shaw

The measure of your life will not be how many breaths you took, but how many breaths you took away.

Anon

The chief danger in life is that you may take too many precautions.

Alfred Adler

It certainly is the duty of every true Christian to esteem himself a stranger and pilgrim in this world; and as bound to use earthly blessings, not as means of satisfying lust or gratifying wantonness, but of supplying his absolute wants and necessities.

Johann Arndt

All life is an experiment. The more experiments you make the better.

Ralph Waldo Emerson

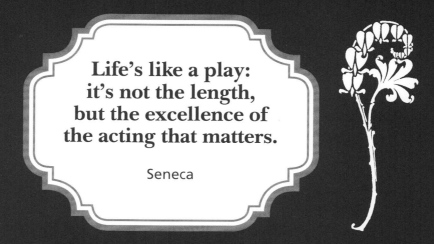

**Life's like a play:
it's not the length,
but the excellence of
the acting that matters.**

Seneca

Believe that life is worth living and your belief will help create the fact.

William James

Do not dwell in the past, do not dream of the future, concentrate the mind on the present moment.

Buddha

*Be who you are and say what you feel because those who
mind don't matter and those who matter don't mind.*

Dr Seuss

Don't grieve for me, for now I'm free!
I follow the plan God laid for me.
I saw His face, I heard His call,
I took His hand and left it all...

Anon

A life of purpose is the purpose of life.

Anon

I have always looked on disobedience toward the oppressive as the only way to use the miracle of having been born.

Oriana Fallaci

In every community, there is work to be done. In every nation, there are wounds to heal. In every heart, there is power to do it.

Marianne Williamson

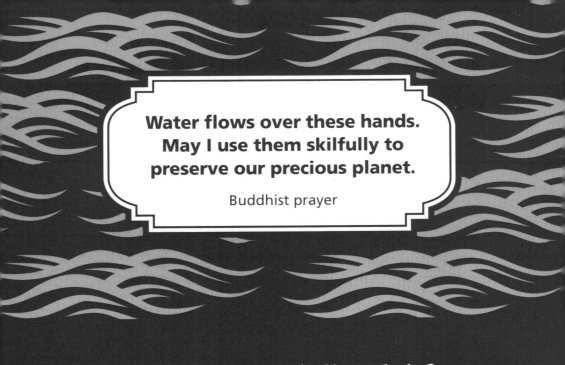

> **Water flows over these hands.**
> **May I use them skilfully to**
> **preserve our precious planet.**
>
> Buddhist prayer

Perhaps my time seemed all too brief,
Don't shorten yours with undue grief.
Be not burdened with tears of sorrow,
Enjoy the sunshine of the morrow.

Anon

No man is a failure who is enjoying life.

William Feather

Our business in life is not to succeed, but to continue to fail in good spirits.

Robert Louis Stevenson

It is a blessed thing that in every age some one has had the individuality enough and courage enough to stand by his own convictions.

Robert G. Ingersoll

If you're alive you've got to flap your arms and legs, you've got to jump around a lot, for life is the very opposite of death and, therefore, you must at the very least think noisily and colourfully, or you're not alive.

Mel Brooks

Many people are alive but don't touch the miracle of being alive.

Thích Nhất Hạnh

Seventy per cent of success in life is showing up.

Woody Allen

It is not length of life, but depth of life.

Ralph Waldo Emerson

Our life is what our thoughts make it.

Marcus Aurelius

The great use of life is to spend it for something that will outlast it.

William James

There is a value to all of us that, if unrecognized by the owner, becomes invisible to the onlooker.

Anon

He who has a why to live can bear almost any how.

Friedrich Nietzsche

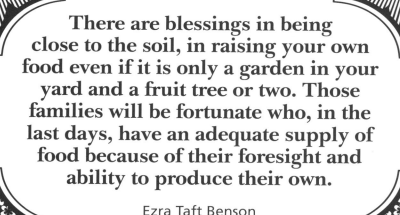

There are blessings in being close to the soil, in raising your own food even if it is only a garden in your yard and a fruit tree or two. Those families will be fortunate who, in the last days, have an adequate supply of food because of their foresight and ability to produce their own.

Ezra Taft Benson

Luck is preparation meeting opportunity.

Oprah Winfrey

Your time is limited, so don't waste it living someone else's life. Don't be trapped by dogma – which is living with the results of other people's thinking. Don't let the noise of others' opinions drown out your own inner voice. And most important, have the courage to follow your heart and intuition.

Steve Jobs

Things won are done, joy's soul lies in the doing.

William Shakespeare

You will never do anything in this world without courage. It is the greatest quality of the mind next to honour.

Aristotle

Who could refrain that had a heart to love and in that heart courage to make love known?

William Shakespeare

> **There are risks and costs to action. But they are far less than the long-range risks of comfortable inaction.**
>
> John F. Kennedy

For a gallant spirit there can never be defeat.

Wallis Simpson

Action may not always bring happiness; but there is no happiness without action.

Benjamin Disraeli

Freedom
of the
Individual

A wise man should consider that health is the greatest of human blessings, and learn how by his own thought to derive benefit from his illnesses.

Hippocrates

It is unwise to be too sure of one's own wisdom. It is healthy to be reminded that the strongest might weaken and the wisest might err.

Mahatma Gandhi

Genius is one per cent inspiration and ninety-nine per cent perspiration.

Thomas A. Edison

Imperfection is beauty, madness is genius and it's better to be absolutely ridiculous than absolutely boring.

Marilyn Monroe

Man, the living creature, the creating individual, is always more important than any established style or system.

Bruce Lee

The gift of fantasy has meant more to me than my talent for absorbing positive knowledge.

Albert Einstein

What is true of the individual will be tomorrow true of the whole nation if individuals will but refuse to lose heart and hope.

Mahatma Gandhi

I submit that an individual who breaks the law that conscience tells him is unjust and willingly accepts the penalty by staying in jail to arouse the conscience of the community over its injustice, is in reality expressing the very highest respect for law.

Martin Luther King, Jr.

**Talent hits a target no one else can hit;
Genius hits a target no one else can see.**

Arthur Schopenhauer

*The ultimate authority must always rest with the
individual's own reason and critical analysis.*

The Dalai Lama

**To be free is not merely to cast off one's
chains, but to live in a way that respects
and enhances the freedom of others.**

Nelson Mandela

Talent perceives differences; genius, unity.

William Butler Yeats

Rightful liberty is unobstructed action according to our will within limits drawn around us by the equal rights of others. I do not add 'within the limits of the law' because law is often but the tyrant's will, and always so when it violates the rights of the individual.

Thomas Jefferson

Remember always that you not only have the right to be an individual, you have an obligation to be one.

Eleanor Roosevelt

People demand freedom of speech as a compensation for the freedom of thought which they seldom use.

Søren Kierkegaard

Freedom prospers when religion is vibrant and the rule of law under God is acknowledged.

Ronald Reagan

Freedom is what you do with what's been done to you.

Jean-Paul Sartre

The only sure bulwark of continuing liberty is a government strong enough to protect the interests of the people, and a people strong enough and well enough informed to maintain its sovereign control over the government.

Franklin D. Roosevelt

Responsibility is the price of freedom.

Elbert Hubbard

Freedom is nothing but a chance to be better.

Albert Camus

I am free because I know that I alone am morally responsible for everything I do. I am free, no matter what rules surround me. If I find them tolerable, I tolerate them; if I find them too obnoxious, I break them. I am free because I know that I alone am morally responsible for everything I do.

Robert A. Heinlein

Freedom is not worth having if it does not connote freedom to err.

Mahatma Gandhi

There are two freedoms: the false, where a man is free to do what he likes; the true, where he is free to do what he ought.

Charles Kingsley

For in the end, freedom is a personal and lonely battle; and one faces down fears of today so that those of tomorrow might be engaged.

Alice Walker

The only freedom which deserves the name is that of pursuing our own good, in our own way, so long as we do not attempt to deprive others of theirs, or impede their efforts to obtain it.

John Stuart Mill

Freedom of opinion can only exist when the government thinks itself secure.

Bertrand Russell

**Real freedom is having nothing.
I was freer when I didn't have a cent.**

Mike Tyson

What is freedom of expression?
Without the freedom to offend,
it ceases to exist.

Salman Rushdie

As long as men are free to ask what
they must, free to say what they think,
free to think what they will, freedom can
never be lost and science can never regress.

Marcel Proust

The revelation of thought takes
men out of servitude into freedom.

Ralph Waldo Emerson

May we think of freedom, not as the right to do as we please, but as the opportunity to do what is right.

Peter Marshall

None who have always been free can understand the terrible fascinating power of the hope of freedom to those who are not free.

Pearl S. Buck

Our freedom can be measured by the number of things we can walk away from.

Vernon Howard

As human beings, we are endowed with freedom of choice, and we cannot shuffle off our responsibility upon the shoulders of God or nature. We must shoulder it ourselves. It is our responsibility.

Arnold J. Toynbee

We must be willing to pay a price for freedom.

H. L. Mencken

Is freedom anything else than the right to live as we wish?

Epictetus

Freedom is the sure possession of those alone who have the courage to defend it.

Pericles

Man is free at the moment he wishes to be.

Voltaire

Freedom is the oxygen of the soul.

Moshe Dayan

Freedom is the only law which genius knows.

James Russell Lowell

It is those who concentrate on but one thing at a time who advance in this world. The great man or woman is the one who never steps outside his or her specialty or foolishly dissipates his or her individuality.

Og Mandino

Freedom is from within.

Frank Lloyd Wright

All theory is against freedom of the will; all experience for it.

Samuel Johnson

You can only protect your liberties in this world by protecting the other man's freedom.

Clarence Darrow

Seek freedom and become captive of your desires. Seek discipline and find your liberty.

Frank Herbert

Certain defects are necessary for the existence of individuality.

Johann Wolfgang von Goethe

Freedom rings where opinions clash.

Adlai E. Stevenson

Resistance to the organized mass can be effected only by the man who is as well organized in his individuality as the mass itself.

Carl Jung

All greatness of character is dependent on individuality. The man who has no other existence than that which he partakes in common with all around him, will never have any other than an existence of mediocrity.

James F. Cooper

If a man is not faithful to his own individuality, he cannot be loyal to anything.

Claude McKay

Individuality is founded in feeling; and the recesses of feeling, the darker, blinder strata of character, are the only places in the world in which we catch real fact in the making, and directly perceive how events happen, and how work is actually done.

William James

The higher mental development of woman, the less possible it is for her to meet a congenial male who will see in her, not only sex, but also the human being, the friend, the comrade and strong individuality, who cannot and ought not lose a single trait of her character.

Emma Goldman

What is genius but the power of expressing a new individuality?

Elizabeth Barrett Browning

Eternal life and the invisible world are only to be sought in God. Only within Him do all spirits dwell. He is an abyss of individuality, the only infinite plenitude.

Karl Wilhelm Friedrich Schlegel

Truth is the property of no individual but is the treasure of all men.

Ralph Waldo Emerson

It is only to the individual that a soul is given.

Albert Einstein

The individual has always had to struggle to keep from being overwhelmed by the tribe. If you try it, you will be lonely often, and sometimes frightened. But no price is too high to pay for the privilege of owning yourself.

Friedrich Nietzsche

Where much is expected from an individual, he may rise to the level of events and make the dream come true.

Elbert Hubbard

God enters by a private door into every individual.

Ralph Waldo Emerson

If you treat an individual... as if he were what he ought to be and could be, he will become what he ought to be and could be.

Johann Wolfgang von Goethe

Few things can help an individual more than to place responsibility on him, and to let him know that you trust him.

Booker T. Washington

If we could give every individual the right amount of nourishment and exercise, not too little and not too much, we would have found the safest way to health.

Hippocrates

There is not one big cosmic meaning for all, there is only the meaning we each give to our life, an individual meaning, an individual plot, like an individual novel, a book for each person.

Anaïs Nin

The community stagnates without the impulse of the individual. The impulse dies away without the sympathy of the community.

William James

Humans are one, not divided, but multiplied into many.

Raheel Farooq

If I were given the opportunity to present a gift to the next generation, it would be the ability for each individual to learn to laugh at himself.

Charles M. Schulz

The liberty of the individual is no gift of civilization.
It was greatest before there was any civilization.

Sigmund Freud

Expose yourself to your deepest fear;
after that, fear has no power, and the
fear of freedom shrinks and vanishes.
You are free.

Jim Morrison

If you love someone, set them free.
If they come back they're yours;
if they don't they never were.

Richard Bach

Those who are free of resentful thoughts surely find peace.

Buddha

If physical death is the price that I must pay to free my white brothers and sisters from a permanent death of the spirit, then nothing can be more redemptive.

Martin Luther King, Jr.

Errors of opinion may be tolerated where reason is left free to combat it.

Thomas Jefferson

When one has the feeling of dislike for evil, when one feels tranquil, one finds pleasure in listening to good teachings; when one has these feelings and appreciates them, one is free of fear.

Buddha

To forgive is to set a prisoner free and discover that the prisoner was you.

Lewis B. Smedes

The person born with a talent they are meant to use will find their greatest happiness in using it.

Johann Wolfgang von Goethe

In giving freedom to the slave, we assure freedom to the free – honourable alike in what we give and what we preserve. We shall nobly save, or meanly lose, the last best hope of earth.

Abraham Lincoln

Where the press is free and every man able to read, all is safe.

Thomas Jefferson

A healthy attitude is contagious but don't wait to catch it from others. Be a carrier.

Tom Stoppard

Common sense is not so common.

Voltaire

Give a man health and a course to steer, and he'll never stop to trouble about whether he's happy or not.

George Bernard Shaw

Don't show off every day, or you'll stop surprising people. There must always be some novelty left over. The person who displays a little more of it each day keeps up expectations, and no one ever discovers the limits of his talent.

Baltasar Gracian

You have a good many little gifts and virtues, but there is no need of parading them, for conceit spoils the finest genius. There is not much danger that real talent or goodness will be overlooked long, and the great charm of all power is modesty.

Louisa May Alcott

Intelligence is the wife, imagination is the mistress, memory is the servant.

Victor Hugo

Everybody needs beauty as well as bread, places to play in and pray in, where nature may heal and give strength to body and soul.

John Muir

If I have seen further it is by standing upon the shoulders of giants.

Isaac Newton

Love and Friendship

If you love everything, you will perceive the divine mystery in things. Once you perceive it, you will begin to comprehend it better every day. And you will come at last to love the whole world with an all-embracing love.

Fyodor Dostoyevsky, *The Brothers Karamazov*

Let us pray that all living beings realize that they are all brothers and sisters, all nourished from the same source of life.

Buddhist prayer

If you live to be a hundred, I want to live to be a hundred minus one day, so I never have to live without you.

A. A. Milne

Friendship is certainly the finest balm for the pangs of disappointed love.

Ralph Waldo Emerson

> **If I had to choose between betraying my country and betraying my friend, I hope I should have the guts to betray my country.**
>
> E. M. Forster

Pain passes, love lasts a lifetime.

Anon

They say there are six degrees of separation between you and another person. However, when people are praying for you there are only two degrees.

Shannon L. Alder

If people are given the chance to experience life in more than one country, they will hate a little less.

Marjane Satrapi

Everything responds to love.

Anon

> **The moment you have in your heart this extraordinary thing called love, and feel the depth, the delight, the ecstasy of it, you will discover that for you the world is transformed.**
>
> J. Krishnamurti

Christ, who has nourished us with himself the living bread, make you one in praise and love, and raise you up at the last day.

Holy Communion blessing

Display a heart of boundless love for all the world.

Buddha

A blessed thing it is for any man or woman to have a friend, one human soul whom we can trust utterly, who knows the best and worst of us, and who loves us in spite of all our faults.

Charles Kingsley

True friends bond in silence.

Anon

Christ the good shepherd, who laid down his life for the sheep, draw you and all who hear his voice, to be one flock within one fold

Holy Communion blessing

May your troubles be less
Your blessings be more.
And nothing but happiness
Come through your door.

Dorien Kelly

May this couple always be the best of friends.

Hindu marriage blessing

May all beings everywhere be happy, peaceful, and free.

Buddha

Lord, make me so pure and strong that all creatures may look upon me with friendship. And may I also look upon all creatures with friendship.

Yajur Veda

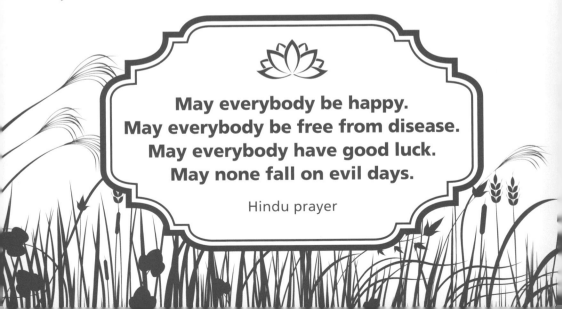

May everybody be happy.
May everybody be free from disease.
May everybody have good luck.
May none fall on evil days.

Hindu prayer

May this couple be blessed with a happy family life.

Hindu marriage blessing

Bless this house, o Lord, we pray.
Make it safe by night and day…
Bless the doors that they may prove
Ever open to joy and love.
Bless the people here within…
Keep them pure and free from sin.
Bless us all, that one day, we
May be fit, O lord, to dwell with Thee.

Prayer

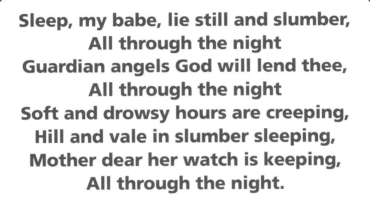

Sleep, my babe, lie still and slumber,
All through the night
Guardian angels God will lend thee,
All through the night
Soft and drowsy hours are creeping,
Hill and vale in slumber sleeping,
Mother dear her watch is keeping,
All through the night.

Irish lullaby

A timely word may level stress but a
loving word may heal and bless.

Anon

A friendship shared, a laugh, a kiss...
Ah yes, these things I, too, shall miss.
My life's been full, I've savoured much:
Good times, good friends, a loved-one's touch.

Anon

Praise be to the Lord of the Universe, who has created us and made us into tribes and nations that we may know each other, not that we may despise each other.

Prayer for peace

May this couple be strong and complement one another.

Hindu marriage blessing

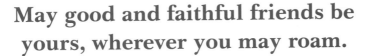

May good and faithful friends be yours, wherever you may roam.

Irish blessing

Help us and save us all, and let us cling tightly to the virtue of peace. Let there be a truly great peace between every person and their fellow, and between husband and wife, and let there be no discord between people even in their hearts.

Jewish prayer

Blessed is the influence of one true, loving human soul on another.

George Eliot

Give us the wisdom to teach our children to love, to respect, and to be kind to each other so that they may grow with peace in mind.

Prayer for peace

These our people; give them good minds to love one another.

Mohawk prayer

For this is one of the miracles of love; it gives – to both, but perhaps especially to the woman – a power of seeing through its own enchantments and yet not being disenchanted.

C. S. Lewis

I have found that if you love life, life will love you back.

Arthur Rubinstein

I just feel very blessed that I found the right person.

Harry Connick, Jr.

I have no doubt concerning that Supreme Goodness, who is so eager to share His blessings, or of that everlasting love which makes Him more eager to bestow perfection on us than we are to receive it.

Saint Ignatius

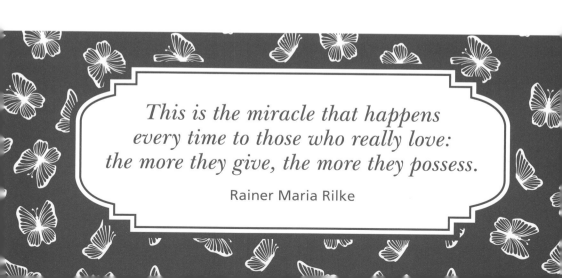

This is the miracle that happens every time to those who really love: the more they give, the more they possess.

Rainer Maria Rilke

The good life is one inspired by love and guided by knowledge.

Bertrand Russell

Beth ceased to fear him from that moment, and sat there talking to him as cosily as if she had known him all her life, for love casts out fear, and gratitude can conquer pride.

Louisa May Alcott, *Little Women*

Life in abundance comes only through great love.

Elbert Hubbard

Love grows with time, but time cannot kill love.

Anon

We fight wars from progressively great heights and distances, the blessings of technology steadily removing the personal human element from what was historically an extremely personal experience.

Steven Weber

We look forward to the time when the Power of Love will replace the Love of Power. Then will our world know the blessings of peace.

William E. Gladstone

To love someone is to see a miracle invisible to others.

François Mauriac

> *One of the greatest titles in the world is parent, and one of the biggest blessings in the world is to have parents to call mom and dad.*
>
> Jim DeMint

The spirit of love unites every heart, blessing the planet with peace.

Anon

The greatest pleasure of life is love.

Euripides

They do not love, that do not show their love.

William Shakespeare

May joy and playful pleasure be yours, may your hopes be fulfilled, and worries never trouble you.

Sikh blessing to a child

We live in the world when we love it.

Rabindranath Tagore

It's a blessed thing to love and feel loved in return.

E. A. Bucchianeri

We all are so deeply interconnected; we have no option but to love all. Be kind and do good for anyone and that will be reflected. The ripples of the kind heart are the highest blessings of the Universe.

Amit Ray

When your children have children it is a double blessing, bringing not only the miracle of new life but also the rebirth of love for your own child.

Anon

A true friend is the greatest of all blessings, and that which we take the least care of all to acquire.

François de La Rochefoucauld

Blessed indeed is the man who hears many gentle voices call him father.

Lydia Maria Francis Child

Blessed are they who have the gift of making friends, for it is one of God's best gifts.

Thomas Hughes

No one is useless in this world who lightens the burdens of another.

Charles Dickens

May your day be touched by a bit of Irish luck, brightened by a song in your heart, and warmed by the smiles of the people you love.

Anon

**Wishing you a rainbow
For sunlight after showers
Miles and miles of Irish smiles
For golden happy hours
Shamrocks at your doorway
For luck and laughter too,
And a host of friends that never ends
Each day your whole life through!**

Irish blessing

*Dreaming ties all
mankind together.*

Jack Kerouac

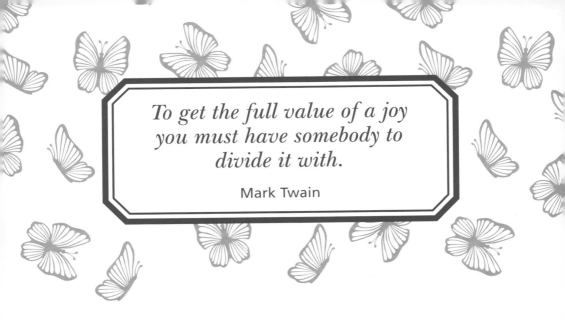

> *To get the full value of a joy*
> *you must have somebody to*
> *divide it with.*
>
> Mark Twain

A man who has been the indisputable favourite of his mother keeps for life the feeling of a conqueror.

Sigmund Freud

As Wind carries our prayers for Earth and All Life, may respect and love light our way.

Buddhist prayer

May the blessed sunlight shine on you and warm your heart until it glows like a great peat fire, so that the stranger may come and warm himself at it, and also a friend.

Irish blessing

Friendship is a single soul dwelling in two bodies.

Aristotle

Walking with a friend in the dark is better than walking alone in the light.

Helen Keller

Love is a better teacher than duty.

Albert Einstein

May the sun always shine on your window pane.
May a rainbow be certain to follow each rain.
May the hand of a friend always be near you.
May God fill your heart with gladness to cheer you.

Irish blessing

Hallow the body as a temple to comeliness and sanctify the heart as a sacrifice to love; love recompenses the adorers.

Khalil Gibran

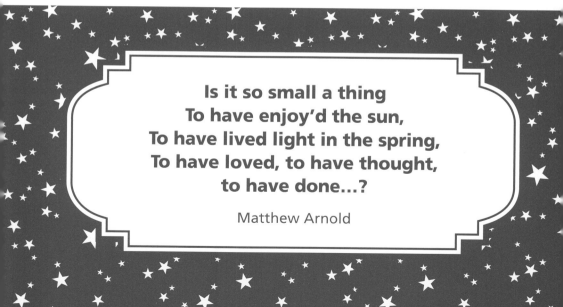

**Is it so small a thing
To have enjoy'd the sun,
To have lived light in the spring,
To have loved, to have thought,
to have done…?**

Matthew Arnold

**Honest good humour is the oil and wine
of a merry meeting, and there is no jovial
companionship equal to that where the jokes
are rather small and laughter abundant.**

Washington Irving

*In all our contacts it is probably
the sense of being really needed
and wanted which gives us the
greatest satisfaction and creates
the most lasting bond.*

Eleanor Roosevelt

You know you're in love when you can't fall asleep because reality is finally better than your dreams.

Dr Seuss

The more one does and sees and feels, the more one is able to do, and the more genuine may be one's appreciation of fundamental things like home, and love, and understanding companionship.

Amelia Earhart

Being deeply loved by someone gives you strength, while loving someone deeply gives you courage.

Lao Tzu

The greatest happiness of life is the conviction that we are loved; loved for ourselves, or rather, loved in spite of ourselves.

Victor Hugo

'Tis better to have loved and lost than never to have loved at all.

Alfred Lord Tennyson

Who, being loved, is poor?

Oscar Wilde

If you enter this world knowing you are loved and you leave this world knowing the same, then everything that happens in between can be dealt with.

Michael Jackson

Love rules the court, the camp, the grove,
And men below, and saints above;
For love is heaven, and heaven is love.

Walter Scott

God bless us, every one!

Charles Dickens

I will only add, God bless you.

Jane Austen

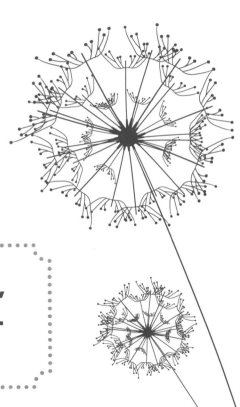

Peace Within, Peace Without

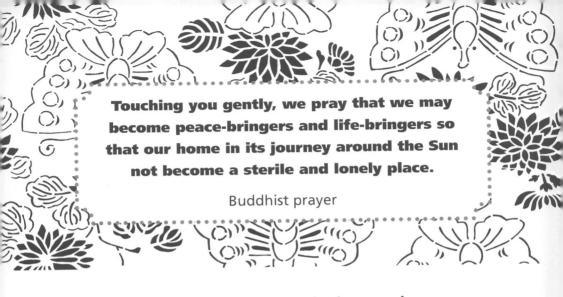

Touching you gently, we pray that we may become peace-bringers and life-bringers so that our home in its journey around the Sun not become a sterile and lonely place.

Buddhist prayer

By whatever name religion may be known, its understanding and practice are the essence of a peaceful mind and therefore of a peaceful world.

The Dalai Lama

If one's mind had peace, the whole world would appear peaceful.

Sri Ramana Maharshi

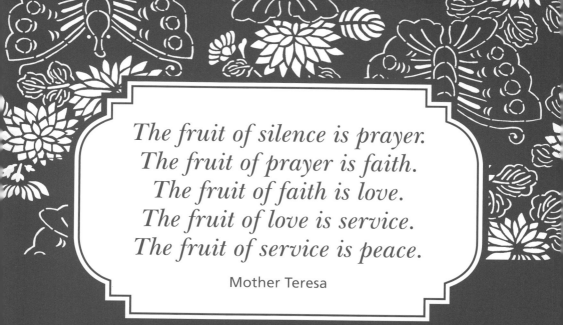

The fruit of silence is prayer.
The fruit of prayer is faith.
The fruit of faith is love.
The fruit of love is service.
The fruit of service is peace.

Mother Teresa

May there be peace in the higher regions;
may there be peace in the firmament;
may there be peace on earth.

Shanti from the Vedas

**May all in this world be happy,
may they be healthy,
may they be comfortable
and never miserable.**

Hindu prayer

**Drink your
tea slowly and
reverently, as if
it is the axis on
which the world
earth revolves.**

Thích Nhất Hạnh

Learn to get in touch with the silence within yourself, and know that everything in life has purpose. There are no mistakes, no coincidences, all events are blessings given to us to learn from.

Elisabeth Kubler-Ross

Holding on to weight (i.e. anger, bitterness, the past, hatred) will not only hold you back, but also block your blessings. You've got to let some things go to move forward.

Yvonne Pierre

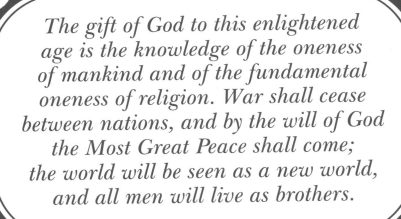

The gift of God to this enlightened age is the knowledge of the oneness of mankind and of the fundamental oneness of religion. War shall cease between nations, and by the will of God the Most Great Peace shall come; the world will be seen as a new world, and all men will live as brothers.

Abdu'l-Baha

May peace increase on Earth.
May it begin with me.

Buddhist prayer

*May the blessing of light be on you –
light without and light within.*

Celtic blessing

Give the greeting of
peace to those one
knows and to those
one does not know.

Islam

**Oh God, You are peace.
From you comes peace, To you returns peace.
Revive us with a salutation of peace,
And lead us to your abode of peace.**

Prophet Muhammad

Through the silence of nature,
I attain thy divine peace.
O sublime nature, in thy
stillness let my heart rest.

Hazrat Inayat Khan

A person must draw strength from
the understanding of the purpose
of creation, rejoicing in advance in
the inevitable reformation of the
entire world and the arrival
of peace for humanity.

Talmud, Truma

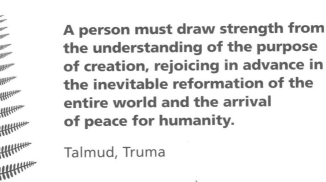

If we are peaceful.
If we are happy.
We can smile and blossom
Like a flower.
And everyone
In our family,
Our entire society
Will benefit
From our peace.

Thích Nhất Hạnh

God who is peace, bless us with peace.

Jewish prayer

May it be thy will to put an end to war and bloodshed on earth, and to spread a great and wonderful peace over the whole world, so that nation shall not lift up sword against nation, neither shall they learn war anymore.

Jewish prayer

There can never be peace between nations until it is first known that true peace is within the souls of men.

Oglala Sioux

Let peace, descending from her native heaven, bid her olives spring amidst the joyful nations; and plenty, in league with commerce, scatter blessings from her copious hand!

Daniel Boone

Life is really simple, but we insist on making it complicated.

Confucius

Happiness is letting go: of negative beliefs, negative emotions and negative people.

Anon

*Better than a thousand hollow words,
is one word that brings peace.*

Buddha

Blest with victory and peace, may the heav'n rescued land Praise the Power that hath made and preserved us a nation.

Francis Scott Key

*If there is to be peace in
the world… there must
be peace in the heart.*

Lao Tzu

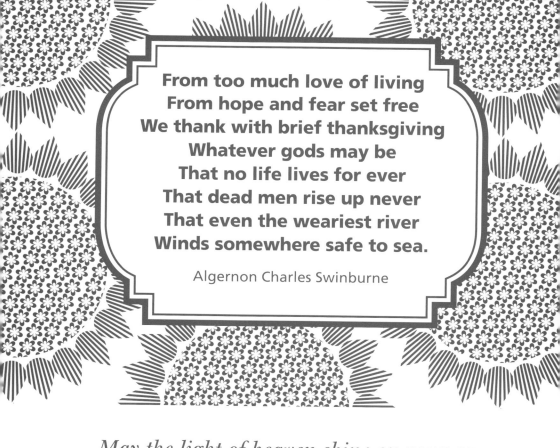

From too much love of living
From hope and fear set free
We thank with brief thanksgiving
Whatever gods may be
That no life lives for ever
That dead men rise up never
That even the weariest river
Winds somewhere safe to sea.

Algernon Charles Swinburne

May the light of heaven shine on your grave.

Irish blessing

**May all beings be peaceful.
May all beings be happy.
May all beings be safe.
May all beings awaken to
the light of their true nature.
May all beings be free.**

Buddhist prayer

*Without inner peace,
there cannot be peace at all.*

Anon

Beware the barrenness of a busy life.

Socrates

Nature does not hurry, yet everything is accomplished.

Lao Tzu

God is the friend of silence.
See how nature – trees, flowers, grass –
grows in silence; see the stars, the moon
and the sun, how they move in silence...
We need silence to be able to touch souls.

Mother Teresa

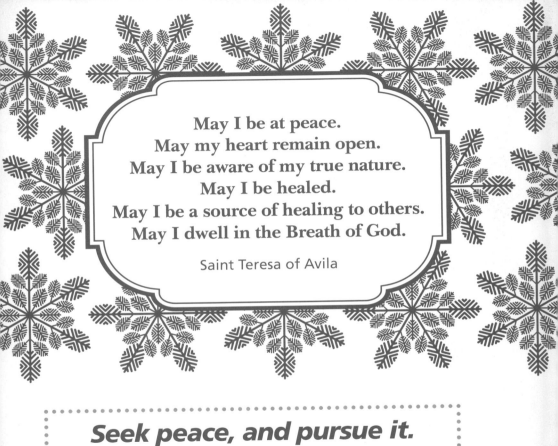

May I be at peace.
May my heart remain open.
May I be aware of my true nature.
May I be healed.
May I be a source of healing to others.
May I dwell in the Breath of God.

Saint Teresa of Avila

Seek peace, and pursue it.

Psalm 34

May peace reign in our hearts, and may we be witnesses to the peace you give to all the world.

Protestant prayer

Only a person at peace with himself can calm others.

Lao Tzu

Peace to all beings, peace among all beings, peace from all beings. I am steeped in peace, absorbed in peace. In the streets, at our work, having peaceful thoughts, peaceful words, peaceful acts.

Buddhist meditation

We reverently pray for eternal
   harmony in the universe.
May the weather be seasonable, may
   the harvest be fruitful,
May countries exist in harmony, and
   may all people enjoy happiness.

Buddhist prayer

May this couple live in perfect harmony…
true to their personal values and their joint promises.

Hindu marriage blessing

Blessed are they who have nothing to say
and who cannot be persuaded to say it.

James Russell Lowell

**Peace be to the East! Peace be to the West!
Peace be to the North! Peace be to the South!
Peace be above! Peace be below!
Peace be to all creatures of this universe!
Peace be everywhere.**

Sri Swami Sivananda

*Never be bullied
into silence.*

Harvey Fierstein

Bless our country, that it may always be a stronghold of peace, and its advocate among the nations. May contentment reign within its borders, health and happiness within its homes.

Christian prayer

The supreme Lord is peace.
May we all be in peace,
peace, and only peace;
and may that peace come
unto each of us.

Shanti from the Vedas

May harmony find you.

Kevin Hearne

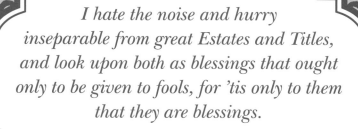

*I hate the noise and hurry
inseparable from great Estates and Titles,
and look upon both as blessings that ought
only to be given to fools, for 'tis only to them
that they are blessings.*

Mary Wortley Montagu

**That we are not much sicker and
much madder than we are is due
exclusively to that most blessed and
blessing of all natural graces, sleep.**

Aldous Huxley

Contentment consists not in adding more fuel, but in taking away some fire.

Thomas Fuller

Walk away. It is not weakness, it is strength. Don't fight to prove your worth, walk away because you already know it.

Anon

Blessed is the man who, having nothing to say, abstains from giving us wordy evidence of the fact.

George Eliot

It is neither wealth nor splendour,
but tranquility and occupation,
which give you happiness.

Thomas Jefferson

He who is of calm and happy nature
will hardly feel the pressure of age,
but to him who is of an opposite
disposition youth and age are
equally a burden.

Plato

Happiness can exist only
in acceptance.

George Orwell

Great tranquillity of heart is his who cares for neither praise nor blame.

Thomas à Kempis

Night, the beloved... When man reassembles his fragmentary self and grows with the calm of a tree.

Antoine de Saint-Exupéry

Great events make me quiet and calm; it is only trifles that irritate my nerves.

Queen Victoria

Motion is tranquillity.

Stirling Moss

God grant me the serenity
to accept the things I cannot
change, the courage to change
the things I can, and the
wisdom to know the difference.

Reinhold Niebuhr

Curiosity endows the people who have it with a generosity in argument and a serenity in their own mode of life which springs from their cheerful willingness to let life take the form it will.

Alistair Cooke

You must be calm before you can utter oracles.

Henry David Thoreau

The art of acceptance is the art of making someone who has just done you a small favour wish that he might have done you a greater one.

Martin Luther King, Jr.

My happiness grows in direct proportion to my acceptance, and in inverse proportion to my expectations.

Michael J. Fox

Acceptance and tolerance and forgiveness, those are life-altering lessons.

Jessica Lange

Chaotic people often have chaotic lives, and I think they create that. But if you try and have an inner peace and a positive outlook, I think you attract that.

Imelda Staunton

There is no end of craving. Hence contentment alone is the best way to happiness. Therefore, acquire contentment.

Swami Sivananda

A man who is not afraid is not aggressive, a man who has no sense of fear of any kind is really a free, a peaceful man.

Jiddu Krishnamurti

If the human race wishes to have a prolonged and indefinite period of material prosperity, they have only got to behave in a peaceful and helpful way toward one another.

Winston Churchill

Wars are poor chisels for carving out peaceful tomorrows.

Martin Luther King, Jr.

As a well spent day brings happy sleep, so a life well spent brings happy death.

Leonardo da Vinci

Death is Nature's way of telling you to slow down.

Anon

Death comes not to the living soul, nor age to the loving heart.

Phoebe Cary

I look upon death to be as necessary to our constitution as sleep. We shall rise refreshed in the morning.

Benjamin Franklin

It is a common experience that a problem difficult at night is resolved in the morning after the committee of sleep has worked on it.

John Steinbeck

Man should forget his anger before he lies down to sleep.

Mahatma Gandhi

Silence is the sleep that nourishes wisdom.

Francis Bacon

The best remedy for those who are afraid, lonely or unhappy is to go outside, somewhere where they can be quiet, alone with the heavens, nature and God. Because only then does one feel that all is as it should be.

Anne Frank

**Blessed are the peacemakers,
for they shall be called
children of God.**

Jesus